POVERTY, U. S. A.

THE HISTORICAL RECORD

ADVISORY EDITOR: David J. Rothman

Professor of History, Columbia University

WHAT IS
SOCIAL CASE WORK?

MARY E. RICHMOND

Arno Press & The New York Times
NEW YORK   1971

Reprint Edition 1971 by Arno Press Inc.

Reprinted by permission of Basic Books, Inc.
Reprinted from a copy in
The Newark Public Library

LC# 70—137185
ISBN 0—405—03123—8

POVERTY, U.S.A.: THE HISTORICAL RECORD
ISBN for complete set: 0-405-03090-8

Manufactured in the United States of America

WHAT IS SOCIAL CASE WORK?

AN INTRODUCTORY DESCRIPTION

By

MARY E. RICHMOND

DIRECTOR, CHARITY ORGANIZATION DEPARTMENT
RUSSELL SAGE FOUNDATION
AUTHOR OF "SOCIAL DIAGNOSIS," "THE GOOD NEIGHBOR," ETC.

NEW YORK
RUSSELL SAGE FOUNDATION
1922

Printed February, 1922, 2549 copies
Reprinted March, 1922, 3000 copies
Reprinted June, 1925, 2000 copies
Reprinted May, 1928, 2000 copies
Reprinted April, 1931, 2000 copies

WM. F. FELL CO., PRINTERS
PHILADELPHIA, PA.

CONTENTS

PAGE

I. INTRODUCTION 5

II. SOCIAL CASE WORK IN BEING . . . 26

III. SOCIAL CASE WORK IN BEING (*Continued*) . 50

IV. SOCIAL CASE WORK DEFINED . . . 87

V. HUMAN INTERDEPENDENCE 126

VI. INDIVIDUAL DIFFERENCES 144

VII. THE BASIS OF PURPOSEFUL ACTION . . 159

VIII. THE HOME 175

IX. SCHOOL—WORKSHOP—HOSPITAL—COURT . 195

X. THE FORMS OF SOCIAL WORK AND THEIR
    INTERRELATIONS 222

XI. CASE WORK AND DEMOCRACY . . . 244

XII. CONCLUSION 255

INDEX 261

3

WHAT IS
SOCIAL CASE WORK?

I

INTRODUCTION

THERE was real teaching in the world long before there was a science or art of teaching; there was social case work long before social workers began, not so many years ago, to formulate a few of its principles and methods. Almost as soon as human beings discovered that their relations to one another had ceased to be primitive and simple, they must have found among their fellows a few who had a special gift for smoothing out the tangles in such relations; they must have sought, however informally, the aid of these "straighteners," as Samuel Butler calls them. Some teachers have had this skill, occasionally ministers of religion have had it, and secular judges, and physicians; though at no time has it been the exclusive possession of these four professions or of any one of them.

A writer whose stories and tales are too little known says of one of her characters:

For the Doctor, in that age of medical darkness, had what is more useful even to his profession than a knowledge of medicine—a great knowledge of character; and was famous for his diagnosis of the maladies of the soul as well as of the body. He not only perceived, which was easy, from the look of Hodge's face and the trembling of his hands, the direction of Hodge's wages; but saw, though indeed only in a glass darkly, what few people saw at all in that day, the effect of mind on body; so that the little dressmaker, a meek, frightened thing, who had set up for herself in Basset . . . required, not physic and plaisters, as she believed, but a start, and an order from Mrs. Latimer at the Manor. The very next afternoon, Dr. Richard wheezed up the Manor drive to see Pollie; obtained her word, which was as good as a bond, to assist Miss Fitten; and cured his patient.*

Even in our own day, the skill of the social case worker who is able to effect better adjustments between the individual and his environment seems to many of us—as reading and

* Tallentyre, S. G.: Basset, A Village Chronicle, p. 93, New York, Moffat, Yard and Co., 1912.

writing seemed to Dogberry—to come by nature. To many, such case work is neighborliness and nothing more. There is a half truth in this neighborliness theory, for the good case worker must be both born and made, but its element of error is the failure to recognize how much is being done in social work to develop a native gift through training and specialized experience.

The difference of method and point of view as between neighbor and specialist is well illustrated in the Life of Laura Bridgman,* where Asa Tenney is the neighbor and Dr. Howe the teacher. Laura, it will be remembered, was the untrained blind and deaf child discovered in 1837 by the Boston philanthropist, Dr. Samuel Gridley Howe, who had founded Perkins Institution for the Blind. For the first time in the history of the deaf-blind, one of their number under his guidance was to learn through touch alone to read and write and use her mind and hands in a variety of occupations. Fortunately, Dr. Howe

* Howe, Maud, and Hall, Florence Howe: Laura Bridgman, Dr. Howe's Famous Pupil and What He Taught Her, p. 34. Boston, Little, Brown and Co., 1903.

had the scientific habit of mind; not only did he devise new ways of releasing an imprisoned spirit, but he kept accurate notes, made at the time, of his methods and results. Upon this foundation, as I shall presently show, others have been able to build.

I have said that the Bridgman family had a neighbor, an old man with a big, simple heart. When Laura was a little girl he used to take her for country walks, and taught her the difference between land and water by letting her feel the splash upon her cheek as she stood by the brookside and threw stones into it. At the time that Dr. Howe asked permission to give Laura systematic instruction, old Asa Tenney was one of those who "scouted the notion of anybody's being able to teach her more than he could. She knew him from anybody else, and she knew a cat from a dog, an apple from a stone, and he could teach her anything in the same way by which she had learned these things."

The world could ill afford to spare its Asa Tenneys. Affection and kindness unlock many doors, straighten out many complications. But when to affection and kindness we are able to add that knowledge of the workings of the human mind and that knowledge of social resources which Dr. Howe possessed, we have a new power in the world added to the older power of just loving one another.

In the year 1886 the parents of a deaf-blind child living in Tuscumbia, Alabama, applied to Perkins Institution for the Blind for a private instructor. Choice fell upon a former pupil of the institution, Anne Mansfield Sullivan,* who had been almost totally blind from early childhood but whose sight had become partially restored before her graduation from the institution. In her student days Miss Sullivan had lived in the same cottage with blind and deaf Laura Bridgman. In addition to her observations of this famous pupil and to her own studies at the school, she was able before going to Tuscumbia to devote a good deal of time, in preparation for her task, to the examination of Dr. Howe's original records and diaries. Thus Dr.

* Now Mrs. Macy.

Howe's stone was cast—not like Laura's into a brook, but into shoreless waters upon which the circles continue to widen and widen.

The story of what followed has been told many times, but not from the angle from which, as an introduction to the subject of case work, I now propose to view it.

Helen Keller was six years and nine months old when Miss Sullivan came to Tuscumbia. Though her teacher did not keep a diary like Dr. Howe's, we have what for my present purpose serves even better. At almost weekly intervals during that first year Miss Sullivan wrote to a friend, the matron of Perkins Institution, giving her not so much the educational details of a task with which her correspondent was already familiar, but describing the new situations, many of them social, with which she found herself confronted, and adding the frankest possible report of her own mental processes in trying to meet these. So we have in the letters not only *what* happened but *how* it happened, and the teacher's own reactions as well as the pupil's.

On the educational side, some of Miss Sullivan's methods anticipate those of the most advanced school of present-day teachers. On the social side, also, they represent at many points our modern social case work method of procedure, though under conditions that social work can seldom command. In 1903 Miss Keller, while a student at Radcliffe College, published The Story of My Life,* and Miss Sullivan's letters are given in Part III of that book. My readers will not be satisfied, I hope, to know anything less than all of these letters, together with the whole book of which they are a part. There could be no better introduction to social case work. In fact, certain incidents in the story are wonderful illustrations of what has been termed unconscious case work, and I shall try to describe a few of these incidents before giving examples of the conscious processes of professional case workers.

Helen had been an "eager, self-asserting" infant. At nineteen months an illness, described as "acute congestion of the stomach and brain,"

* Keller, Helen: The Story of My Life. New York, Doubleday, Page and Co.

had left her deaf and blind. She was learning to talk before the attack, but very shortly "ceased to speak because she could not hear." Soon she began to tyrannize over everybody, "her mother, her father, the servants, the little darkies who play with her, and nobody," wrote Miss Sullivan, "had ever seriously disputed her will, except occasionally her brother James, until I came." The parents gave the new teacher entire charge of the little girl.

They have promised to let me have a free hand and help me as much as possible. . . Of course, it is hard for them. I realize that it hurts to see their afflicted little child punished and made to do things against her will. Only a few hours after my talk with Captain and Mrs. Keller (and they had agreed to everything) Helen took a notion that she wouldn't use her napkin at table. I think she wanted to see what would happen. I attempted several times to put the napkin round her neck; but each time she tore it off and threw it on the floor and finally began to kick the table. I took her plate away and started to take her out of the room. Her father objected and said that no child of his should be deprived of his food on any account. (p. 313)*

* Page references throughout this summary are to passages in Miss Keller's The Story of My Life.

Thus Miss Sullivan had the task of winning over more than one insurgent. This was in March. By the following Christmas she was able to write:

. . . It was evident that every one, especially Captain and Mrs. Keller, was deeply moved at the thought of the difference between this bright Christmas and the last, when their little girl had no conscious part in the Christmas festivities. As we came downstairs, Mrs. Keller said to me with tears in her eyes, "Miss Annie, I thank God every day of my life for sending you to us; but I never realized until this morning what a blessing you have been to us." Captain Keller took my hand, but could not speak. But his silence was more eloquent than words. My heart, too, was full of gratitude and solemn joy. (pp. 343–44)

How was this transformation effected? Cut off from the normal approaches to a child's heart, Miss Sullivan had very early had a frank talk with Mrs. Keller and suggested that Helen be separated from her family for a few weeks. There were "two essential things to teach her, obedience and love," and neither could be taught without a chance to pursue a consistent, uninterrupted policy. Accordingly, teacher and pupil were established in a little garden house near the former Keller home. At that time Helen "was unresponsive and even impatient of caresses from any one except her mother." In the new surroundings she "was greatly excited at first, and kicked and screamed herself into a sort of stupor. . . . When she felt me get into bed with her, she jumped out on the other side." (p. 310)

Captain Keller came every day, unknown to Helen, to see how his little daughter was progressing. He often found her crocheting a long red chain of Scotch wool or stringing beads on a sewing-card, and he remarked how quiet and contented she seemed. One day, during the two weeks of Helen's separation from her family, his dog, Belle, came too. The child recognized the dog's presence and, sitting down beside her, began to manipulate her claws. "We couldn't think for a second," writes Miss Sullivan, "what she was doing; but when we saw her make the letters 'd-o-l-l' on her own fingers, we knew that she was trying to teach Belle to spell." (p. 313) Helen's teacher had been spelling whole words into the child's hand without instructing her

14

in the manual alphabet, and had associated this spelling with the corresponding objects.

Tempting as are the passages in Miss Sullivan's letters which describe her extensions and modifications of Dr. Howe's great educational discovery, the matter to which I must confine myself here is the use that she made of Helen's own world—not only of her immediate household but of the social occasions of the community, the animal life of the farm, and the beauty and variety of the whole countryside.

Laura Bridgman had not only been trained in an institution as a child, but had found in it her only satisfactory home as long as she lived, dying there in her sixtieth year. Helen Keller on the contrary, was to become a citizen of the world. As every one knows, she was graduated from Radcliffe College, has written several books, is interested in the education of the deaf-blind, and has had the deep satisfaction of winning for them many better opportunities. Her social endeavors have not stopped here, however, but have been extended to the much larger group of all the blind, and she has also been an active

champion of woman's suffrage and of other
social reforms. That Miss Keller was born with
great natural endowment is obvious, but she
herself has always been the first to proclaim that
Miss Sullivan's ability to make her education a
social one, Miss Sullivan's genius for ignoring
routine and for using life itself as her best in-
terpreter has meant the difference between a
singularly happy life and one of utter wretched-
ness.

It is from an embarrassing wealth of material
that I choose the brief quotations following, of
which the first illustrates Miss Sullivan's use of
the animals on the Keller plantation in developing the mind of her charge; the second illustrates
her way of making the whole household parti-
cipants in the process; the third, her skill in
turning a community occasion to account; and
the fourth, her recognition of the part that nature
could play. The animals were early pressed into
service.

She is much interested in some little chickens that
are pecking their way into the world this morning. I
let her hold a shell in her hand, and feel the chicken

"chip, chip." Her astonishment, when she felt the tiny creature inside, cannot be put in a letter. The hen was very gentle, and made no objection to our investigations. Besides the chickens, we have several other additions to the family—two calves, a colt, and a penful of funny little pigs. You would be amused to see me hold a squealing pig in my arms, while Helen feels it all over, and asks countless questions—questions not easy to answer either. (p. 325)

We go home about dinner-time usually, and Helen is eager to tell her mother everything she has seen. *This desire to repeat what has been told her shows a marked advance in the development of her intellect, and is an invaluable stimulus to the acquisition of language. I ask all her friends to encourage her to tell them of her doings, and to manifest as much curiosity and pleasure in her little adventures as they possibly can.* This gratifies the child's love of approbation and keeps up her interest in things. This is the basis of real intercourse. She makes many mistakes, of course, twists words and phrases, puts the cart before the horse, and gets herself into hopeless tangles of nouns and verbs; but so does the hearing child. I am sure these difficulties will take care of themselves. The impulse to tell is the important thing. (pp. 321–22)

It is interesting to get Miss Keller's impressions as well as her teacher's of that memorable year. She writes:

The first Christmas after Miss Sullivan came to Tuscumbia was a great event. Every one in the family prepared surprises for me; but what pleased me most, Miss Sullivan and I prepared surprises for everybody else. The mystery that surrounded the gifts was my greatest delight and amusement. My friends did all they could to excite my curiosity by hints and half-spelled sentences which they pretended to break off in the nick of time.

On Christmas Eve the Tuscumbia school children had their tree, to which they invited me. In the centre of the schoolroom stood a beautiful tree ablaze and shimmering in the soft light, its branches loaded with strange, wonderful fruit. It was a moment of supreme happiness. I danced and capered round the tree in an ecstasy. When I learned that there was a gift for each child, I was delighted, and the kind people who had prepared the tree permitted me to hand the presents to the children. In the pleasure of doing this, I did not stop to look at my own gifts; but when I was ready for them, my impatience for the real Christmas to begin almost got beyond control. (p. 41)

All my early lessons have in them the breath of the woods—the fine, resinous odour of pine needles, blended with the perfume of wild grapes . . . Indeed, everything that could hum, or buzz, or sing, or bloom, had a part in my education—noisy-throated frogs, katydids and crickets held in my hand until, forgetting their embarrassment, they trilled their reedy note, little downy chickens and wildflowers, the dogwood blossoms, meadow-violets and budding fruit trees. I felt the bursting cotton-bolls and

fingered their soft fiber and fuzzy seeds; I felt the low
soughing of the wind through the cornstalks, the silky
rustling of the long leaves, and the indignant snort of my
pony, as we caught him in the pasture and put the bit in
his mouth . . . (pp. 34–35)

Then came Helen's introduction to a larger
range of social contacts, first through her visit
to Perkins Institution, and later through instruction in New York and Cambridge.

[First visit to Boston.] I was never still a moment;
my life was as full of motion as those little insects that
crowd a whole existence into one brief day. I met many
people who talked with me by spelling into my hand, and
thought in joyous sympathy leaped up to meet thought,
and behold, a miracle had been wrought! The barren
places between my mind and the minds of others blossomed
like the rose. (p. 50)

At the Cambridge school, for the first time in my life, I
enjoyed the companionship of seeing and hearing girls of
my own age. I lived with several others in one of the
pleasant houses connected with the school, the house
where Mr. Howells used to live, and we all had the advantage of home life. I joined them in many of their games,
even blind man's buff and frolics in the snow; I took long
walks with them; we discussed our studies and read aloud
the things that interested us. Some of the girls learned to
speak to me, so that Miss Sullivan did not have to repeat
their conversation. (pp. 86–87)

At Tuscumbia there had been no one to whom Miss Sullivan could turn in perplexity; she had been thrown upon her own resources and had been forced to work out her own solution of each difficulty as best she could. But when her pupil was able to travel, no teacher could have been more eager to use expert advice and assistance wherever these could be found. Helen heard, for instance, in 1890 of a Norwegian deaf and blind girl who had been taught to speak, and she entreated her teacher to find such instruction for her. Although Miss Sullivan dreaded for her charge the disappointment of a possible failure, she did not hesitate long, but took Helen to a specialist in New York from whom she could gain the rudiments of articulation. Carefully heeding the methods used by this expert, Miss Sullivan was able to supplement the special training. But for her genius, untiring perseverance and devotion, as Miss Keller testifies, "I could never have progressed as far as I have toward natural speech."

Again, in the matter of religious instruction, Helen's teacher sought the aid of Bishop Brooks.

INTRODUCTION

As a child [Miss Keller says] I loved to sit on his knee and clasp his great hand with one of mine, while Miss Sullivan spelled into the other his beautiful words about God and the spiritual world. I heard him with a child's wonder and delight. My spirit could not reach up to his, but he gave me a real sense of joy in life, and I never left him without carrying away a fine thought that grew in beauty and depth of meaning as I grew. Once, when I was puzzled to know why there were so many religions, he said: "There is one universal religion, Helen—the religion of love. Love your Heavenly Father with your whole heart and soul, love every child of God as much as ever you can, and remember that the possibilities of good are greater than the possibilities of evil; and you have the key to Heaven." (pp. 133–34)

Finally, to bring these extracts to an end, there is abundant evidence that one of the elements in Miss Sullivan's success was the great frankness with which she habitually treated Helen after her confidence had been won. Her resemblances to normal folk were always emphasized; the differences which might so easily have set her apart were minimized. This policy the teacher impressed upon others who came in contact with her pupil.

No attempt [says the editor of Miss Keller's Life] is

made by those around her either to preserve or to break her illusions. When she was a little girl, a good many unwise and tactless things that were said for her benefit were not repeated to her, thanks to the wise watchfulness of Miss Sullivan. Now that she has grown up, nobody thinks of being less frank with her than with any other intelligent young woman. (p. 294)

Let me summarize this illustration of unconscious case work in a few words and try at the same time to suggest some of its resemblances to the conscious case work which is to be described later. This remarkable teacher had a true instinct for that greatest of all realities—the reality of personality. Beneath all the handicaps of her charge and the unfortunate effects of those handicaps she was able to divine the unusual character of the child. Building upon this discovery, she summoned one environmental resource after another, first to release, then to develop, that highly socialized personality of whom we speak today when we name Helen Keller.

Almost from the beginning it was possible to push beyond the negative side of the task. The preliminary lesson in childish obedience was necessary to orderly progress, and once learned, Helen's affection was soon won. To accomplish this, however, Miss Sullivan took upon herself the humblest duties, such as dispensing with a nurse for Helen and caring for her personally until she was able to care for herself. Here again the instructor was too wise to build upon influence gained through one channel, whether obedience or affection. Soon she was able to appeal to the mind of her pupil—doing this through everything in the child's world, even through the very persons and things that seemed at first to be obstacles in her path.

There is a sympathy, an affection, which makes us feel strong; there is another which makes us dependent and weak. Miss Sullivan's sympathy *released* her pupil from that dependence, and it did this by establishing her relation to a multitude of vital, growing things and ideas, first in space, later in time. One of the most pitifully isolated of human beings thus became one of the most completely identified with whatever is best in the world.

I shall have occasion to refer repeatedly in

these pages to change of environment as a means of social treatment in difficult cases. In the first month of her teaching, Miss Sullivan used this particular means so skilfully that it was possible to return Helen to her own natural world at the end of only two weeks.

Another mark of Miss Sullivan's intuitive social work sense was her willingness to turn to any one whose expert knowledge of whatever kind could supplement her own. She was wisely humble, for example, about Helen's ambition to learn to speak, and about the child's spiritual needs. Trained herself in a school which did not attempt to teach articulation to the deaf-blind, she felt a certain skepticism and she overcame it. In the matter of Helen's religious training she recognized both the urgency and the extreme delicacy of the task, and turned for aid to one of the greatest religious teachers of that time.

Finally, she taught her charge to trust her absolutely by being worthy of that trust. In the service of personality—of a personality other than our own—there is a field of endeavor, whether we call it teaching or social case work or by some other title, that is of all fields the most exacting. We àre "named and known" by such service; by and through it we take our "station and degree."

II

SOCIAL CASE WORK IN BEING

IT MAY be well, before attempting any description of social case work as practised in a genuinely professional spirit, to present some illustrations of such work and later compare illustrations with description. The purpose of this small book is not, however, to discuss method, but to inquire into *what* social case work is and *why* it is.

The typical character of any group of examples can be challenged, of course, especially when the group is perforce so small as is the one here selected, but the process by which I arrived at a choice is as follows: After discarding, in my search, all work not recorded with a fair degree of fulness at the time that it was done, I have given preference to those social case records which covered a period of active treatment varying from two to six years, and preference to work with clients* of different nationalities. The search was made in cities widely separated and in social agencies of more than one type, though I have had to exclude agencies in which the social treatment was subsidiary to some other form of professional service. To these limitations I have added the further one of an arbitrary choice of the following general types of problem:

A difficult, maladjusted girl who is not a defective

A small boy in need of a home

A husband and wife who cannot agree

A fatherless family with children who are not receiving proper care

A widow with children who is not an efficient home maker

An older woman with difficulties which her relatives fail to understand

* Few social case workers adopt the practice, permitted to the physician, of referring to those with whom they have professional dealings as "cases." The social worker's "case" is the particular social situation or problem—not the person or persons concerned. For the person, as distinguished from his problem, the term now in general use is "client." As the nature of the relation between the social practitioner and the one receiving social treatment changed,

WHAT IS SOCIAL CASE WORK?

I have mentioned Dr. Howe's diary records of his treatment of Laura Bridgman. As social workers have gradually learned how to render more intelligent and effective service to individuals and families, Dr. Howe's practice of keeping a record of developments in treatment has become their practice also. At first their attempts were little more than a rambling chronicle of motions made in the course of their work, but gradually they have learned how to construct good, chronological accounts both of the essential processes used and of the observations upon which these processes were based. A record so made becomes not only an indispensable guide to future action in behalf of the person recorded; it can be unexcelled material for training other case workers, and for training those who, in preparation for other types of social work—such as work with neighborhood groups or social research or the conducting of social reform campaigns—seek a clearer understanding of the numberless ways in which bad

"client" replaced to a large extent the earlier term of "applicant."

social conditions affect the lives of individuals. The value of social case records extends farther. Under analysis which is thoroughly competent and careful they may become the basis of statistical studies or, more often, of social discovery arrived at by non-statistical methods.

There is one drawback to all these uses of the social case history. In the whole range of professional contacts there is no more confidential relation than that which exists between the social worker and the person or family receiving treatment. But unfortunately a social history is far more easily identified with the person or persons whose private affairs it records than is any other form of record—than the medical case history, for example. It will not be necessary, however, to report the problems here presented with anything like the fulness required for purposes of training or of research. My own quest is confined to narrow limits, the one aim being to reveal what social case work in its essentials is. It has been possible, therefore, not only greatly to foreshorten the narratives of these few selected records, but, by deliberately changing a number of their details when these had no relation to the problems and services described, to conceal still further the identity of the originals.

During the last decade social case work has had a rapid extension of its field of activity. At one time, as a vocation, its field was confined almost exclusively to the care of dependents and delinquents, just as the first savings banks were for dependents only and the first hospitals for the destitute sick. But today social case work in some form or other has become a necessary part of many of our courts, schools, hospitals, factories, workshops, compensation commissions, and of the hundred other places in which decisions affecting the welfare of individuals must be made. In many of these places, however, the habit of full recording is not yet well established, and the work has been organized so recently that long-continued service to the same individuals or families, with its surer measure of successes and failures, is still the exception. It is for these reasons that I have confined my choice of illustrations to the longer established children's societies and family welfare societies.

So much by way of explanation. Having selected a record, my first care has been to study it in detail before conferring with the case worker who made it. After full conference I have prepared my own account, with many details of the history omitted and the case worker's plans and policies emphasized. Finally, I have submitted my account to the case worker for revision and correction. Some of these precautions may have been unnecessary, but at least they will have saved me from becoming just one more narrator of moving little stories. The six narrative accounts that immediately follow, unpicturesque though they are, deserve a more careful reading than the discussion which later grows out of them.

MARIA BIELOWSKI*

My first illustration of "case work in being" describes the social treatment given for four

* All names of real people have been changed throughout these narratives, as well as some other identifying but non-essential details.

years to a Polish girl, who was under the care of a small private society having a staff of case workers and a school for difficult but not defective young girls. From this school its pupils are usually placed out in private families, where they continue to be under the careful supervision of the society's staff. Before the girl whose story I shall tell entered the school, she had been the charge for a short while of a probation officer of the court.

Maria Bielowski went to work in a factory when she was only fifteen. After many disagreements with her stepmother about the share of her wages to be turned over to the family and also about her habit of staying out late at night, she left home and began to live in lodging houses and cheap hotels. From one of these the girl was brought into court for stealing a few dollars from a fellow-boarder. To those who saw her just after her arrest she was a very unprepossessing sight. Her features were dark and heavy, her clothing ragged, dirty, and badly stained; her head was crowned with three strands of false hair, later found to be infested with vermin.

What did the probation officer discover as to her background? From two places of employment her record was that of an irregular worker. One hospital asked to examine her reported that she had good intellectual capacity but a psychopathic personality. As regards her family, the Bielowskis had come from Poland five years earlier—the father, his second wife, and four children. But the father had died three years after his arrival, and the stepmother, who could speak not a dozen English words, appeared, although a good woman, to have lost all control over the children. The two grown sons were away from home; the younger boy was in a reformatory. Should Maria, who had been found guilty by the court, be committed to a similar institution?

The social data obtained by the probation officer made it appear unwise to place the girl on probation in her own home. On the other hand, her record before she had gone to work did not seem to justify commitment to a reformatory. At school she had been a fair scholar; beginning with no knowledge of English whatever, she had completed the seventh grade in four years. Moreover, it was learned that she had been a popular member of a Girl Scout troop and of her Sunday school class. These facts suggested that probation under conditions which would assure a maximum of individualized care might bring good results. Accordingly, the officer sought the aid of the small private society already mentioned, and somewhat later, after Maria had been in its school a few months, one of their case workers became, with the sanction of the girl, the girl's family, and the court, her legal guardian. Under this guardianship her behavior and character have improved steadily.

From a careful reading in the original record of the treatment which followed and from conference with this guardian, I have been able to trace some of the steps by which the marked change in the girl's habits and in her relations to the world she lives in has been effected. There has been no element of the magical or the spectacular in her gradual development.

During the earlier stages of treatment careful

attention had to be given to Maria's physical condition. Her scalp was cleansed and her teeth cared for. There was no evidence of irregular sex conduct, but she was found to have some symptoms of syphilis of origin unknown, and was taken regularly into the city for hospital treatments. A bad nose and throat condition was treated at the same hospital. Enuresis was controlled at the school by suggestion. Twice during the following year, at times of special discouragement, this symptom recurred, but it responded at once to any change of program which improved her mental attitude. Her other physical difficulties were soon remedied.

It was at the society's little school, with its less than twenty pupils, that Maria had her first contact with American standards of home life. Here she was given careful training in habits of personal cleanliness, in the care of her room, in mending and washing her clothing, in cooking, and in respect for the personal belongings of others. No borrowing was allowed; each girl had her own bureau and closet and her own small treasures. One day early in her stay, two

35

little cakes from a new baking were missing from the kitchen pantry. Every girl denied taking them, so the whole group were deprived of their Christmas trip to town. Three days later Maria confessed to the head teacher, for whom she had learned to have a real affection, that she was the one at fault, and this was her last dishonest act. In one of the private homes in which she worked a year or two later, her employer reported her to be so honest that "she would not even borrow an ink bottle."

After eight months in the school and her completion of the eighth grade, Maria was sent as a mother's helper to a family at a summer resort. In the autumn of that year a position was found for her in another family, to help with the housework in exchange for her board and with the opportunity to enter the first-year class at the high school. She has continued her high school course with credit ever since, making one change of school, however, when transferred to another city. Here there was a chance to place her with a Polish professor and his wife, in whose family she has had many advantages in addition to her pleasure at being once more with compatriots. Each summer the society finds a place for her amid country surroundings, and each year it has arranged a vacation, once at a girls' camp. During the four years under guardianship she has worked in five different families. Though only two of the frequent changes were due to her own restlessness, Maria has at times been a troublesome charge, eager and demanding and inordinately fond of personal adornment.

These family placements, which were all made with the greatest care, have been valuable in giving the girl a chance to participate in American life and ways, but the most important influence in her improvement has continued to be that of the case worker appointed as her guardian. Without dwelling upon details, let me try to name some of the principles and processes of case work that Maria's history reveals.

Probably the case worker's ability to win her way with a difficult girl was due more to her imaginative sympathy than to any other one thing. But whether this quality was a native endowment or partly a result of experience with

other girls, the outstanding fact of the record is
that the guardian did contrive to see the world
in somewhat the fashion that it appeared to her
ward. Having some of the dangers of her own
professional world in mind, perhaps, she was also
careful to avoid that rigidity of mind, that
tendency to inhibit the client's initiative, which
is the too common reaction to irritating behavior. Thus she writes in a letter of explanation:

> Whenever I can possibly let a girl do what she wants to,
> I agree to her doing it. The instances are so innumerable
> where we have to say "no" that I feel we must be on our
> guard against increasing them unnecessarily. This is not
> the same thing as giving in to a girl because she teases or
> insists on having her own way.

When Maria was troublesome, her guardian
discriminated between the trouble that she
caused and the real delinquency of which she
had been, but was no longer, guilty. Her appeal
was constantly to the girl's self-respect and ambition, though not so much in set terms as in
acts which would stimulate these qualities. The
society had Maria's earlier trials in mind when

it allowed her a little more pocket-money than was granted to some of its other charges. Her clothes were never satisfactory to her; after a few months she tired of every purchase, no matter how much it pleased her at first. At one time the question of clothing versus schooling became so acute that she was given permission to leave school and take a short course which would fit her for office work. But when the girl actually realized that the break with school would be permanent, she changed her mind and asked permission to remain.

One day Maria received a circular from a distant city offering, through a course of lessons by mail, to give her a perfect speaking and singing voice. The fee was $50. She applied at once to her guardian for the loan of the money, and was told that the next time they were both in the city they could consult some one whose knowledge of music would make him a good judge of the value of the offer. A teacher at a good music school was asked to test her voice and give an opinion of the plan. When Maria heard the small, wavering sounds that she made in trying to sing to the master, even she was convinced that the correspondence course was not worth considering.

Another way in which arbitrariness was avoided by this case worker was to assume no superhuman perfection in herself. She did not insist upon her own infallibility in homely matters any more than she had in musical ones. Thus she writes:

> I can remember speaking to Maria about mending her clothes, particularly her stockings, and becoming conscious at the moment of a long rent in my own stocking, which I had torn that morning in putting it on and had not had time to change. I laughed and showed the rent to the girl, and spoke of my own difficulty in living up to my ideals when pressed by work. From what she afterward said about this to some one else I know that I carried my point with more effect by this admission.

Closely related to this habit of introducing an element of give and take even into her admonitions, and bringing to mind Miss Sullivan's policy, was the case worker's determination to be honest and frank—to give the real reason for a decision wherever this was possible.

Maria questioned me one day in my earlier contacts with her about her trips to the hospital for treatment. I told her about syphilis, about the fact that the hospital had never been willing to state whether her case was congenital or acquired in very early infancy. I stated that the usual causes of syphilis were promiscuity and exposure to an infected person, and also spoke of the possibility of accidental infection.

This habit of giving the true answer to questions did not mean that the guardian always told all she knew as soon as she knew it. On the contrary, she found that Maria's respect increased for her when she proved to be hard to deceive, when she was able occasionally to surprise her charge by a piece of information supposed to be undiscovered. To give all the freedom that by any chance her ward could make right use of, but to give this freedom under such conditions that she herself could get a pretty clear idea of what that use was, had proved the best policy. At one time, for instance, a young Pole appeared on the scene whom Maria threatened to marry unless she could have a new hat at once. By a judicious arrangement with her employer covering permitted calls and attentions from this young man, and by providing clothing in due season and not before, the small crisis was successfully passed.

This case worker's wise handling of Maria, however, all comes back to the gift of imaginative sympathy, such as was shown when she sent one of the girl's class compositions to a periodical for young people. The composition was accepted by the editor with a small payment in return, and its acceptance meant a great deal to the young writer.

One cannot help wondering what Maria would be like today if the court had treated the fact of larceny in a merely routine way, without taking into account the social background brought to light by the probation officer, and had pronounced the usual sentence for that particular offense. A very different girl would now be crossing the threshold into womanhood— untruthful, hard, perhaps depraved. As it is, she faces the future with the advantages of a high school education, with good health, an attractive personality, and a number of real friends who trust her. She is not a perfect mortal, of course; she is still somewhat restless at times, still magnifies the importance of trifles, and is still too fond of finery. But on the whole her sense of values is an adjusted sense; her ideas are no longer confused and unreasonable.

GEORGE FOSTER

A young American, little George Foster, had been placed with his sister in an institution for children and then had been returned to his parents no less than four times in five years. Even under favorable circumstances these repeated changes of environment are bad for children, but the home to which George and his sister went back was not really a home at all. The father was a drunken bully who worked irregularly; the mother was promiscuous sexually; the pair were not even married. When they quarreled and fought, as they often did, children and household were neglected.

Finally, acting upon a request from the local overseer of the poor, a child-placing society which had its headquarters many miles away from the Foster family undertook to find a free home for both children.*

In selecting such a home, the family's reason for wanting a child and their plans for his education and future are very carefully gone into by the case workers of the society, who also study the make-up of the household, the characteristics and health of each member, and the relation of each to all the others. The family finances have to be known, the physical characteristics and surroundings of the home, together with the family's standing in their neighborhood and community, and their church affiliations. In fact, the study of a home about to receive a child calls for no small degree of social experience. Good placement usually provides a dependent child without even one responsible parent with the best possible chance of

* A "free home" is one in a private family, where the placed-out child becomes a member of the household whether or not its legal adoption is contemplated; the term distinguishes this type of home from a "boarding home," where the family receives compensation for the child's care, and from "working homes," such as the households in which Maria Bielowski lived while she attended school.

44

well-being and development, whereas careless, un-
intelligent placement gives him no chance at all.

The first placement of the Foster children was
not wholly successful. It was with plain farmer
folk. The farmer's wife was not in good health,
and the care of two children might have been a
burden to her under any circumstances, though
the chief difficulty was in the relation of the two
children to one another. Following the practice
of their parents, perhaps, they quarreled continually, thus bringing out each other's worst
qualities and irritating their foster mother.
George was nine at this time, an affectionate
but high-tempered child, whereas his sister,
nearly three years his senior, had all the characteristics of a self-assertive, middle-aged gossip.
Consequently, after several visits by the society's agent to the farm and to the nearby
school that the children attended, it was decided
to remove both children and place them separately. This latter decision was not made lightly;
it was contrary to the society's usual policy.
From this point George's story is the only one
that I shall attempt to follow. He was deeply

distressed at the thought of leaving the farm, but the visitor encouraged him to talk about all the things he had enjoyed there—the hay making, the chickens, the garden—and made him realize that he was not parting with these pleasures for good.

At this time George was brought to the city in which the children's society had its headquarters, and advantage was taken of this opportunity to study the child's needs more carefully than had been possible earlier. He was given a thorough physical and mental testing and was found to have good native capacity. At a temporary home where the child was placed under expert observation for a while, he was reported to have a stubborn streak, but "when he once understands that he can gain nothing by his bad temper, he will be a very sweet, attractive little boy. . . . He is happy most of the time, and gets over his 'bad times' much more quickly than he did at first."

In a few months it was felt by the society that George was ready for another free home. This time an application had come from a childless couple living in the outskirts of a small town, who had adopted a boy of seven and wished to take another somewhat older. On visiting this home the society's field agent was careful to keep in mind the adopted child's probable attitude toward a foster brother. She also visited fellow-townsmen given as references, and, when these proved satisfactory, gave the family a chance to make a tentative choice among several available boys whose pictures she was able to show. George's picture was the one selected, and further details about him were sent by mail. Soon he was established in this new home. In the case worker's visits to him there she gave each of his foster parents ample opportunity to talk over recent developments and difficulties, and afterwards saw George separately and visited his school. During all these visits there were adjustments to be made between George and the adopted child and between George and his foster father.

This was in the influenza year. The boy had a bad attack of the disease, which left him with a cough and tubercular infection. The society's field worker repeatedly visited his doctor during this time. Gradually the condition in George's lungs cleared up. Meanwhile, his foster parents, though good to him, began to feel, for financial and other reasons, that the care being given to this second boy prevented their doing all that they wished to do for their adopted son, and once again it became necessary for the society to uproot their young charge. Allowing for the many changes, he had done fairly well in school. By the time he was twelve he had made the fifth grade.

The third free home has proved a much happier place for George Foster than any he has yet known in his brief but somewhat stormy career. He has lived for more than a year now in the family of a professional man in which there are several young people but no other children. At first they thought they could not keep him; he was not always respectful to his elders and was not doing well in school. But he was old enough to be reasoned with and, in an admirable interview with him, the case worker succeeded in taking him into partnership in the task of straightening out his relations both with the members of the household and with his teachers. Meanwhile, the family were persuaded to adopt less exacting standards of what a boy of twelve should be expected to enjoy in the matter of improving literature. Ever since this pivotal visit there has been steady improvement in George's behavior and enhanced appreciation on the part of his foster parents of his good points. His health is now excellent. He seems to have a special aptitude for music, and recently has been taking music lessons.

III

SOCIAL CASE WORK IN BEING
(Continued)

THE illustrations given in the preceding chapter are of case work confined to one individual. It was necessary, of course, to win the co-operation of the families in which Maria Bielowski and George Foster were placed, and it was necessary during treatment to utilize the skill of experts of various kinds, but Maria was removed from her own home and did not return to it, while not only was George permanently separated from his own people but, when he and his sister could not agree, he was placed in a separate home. The case workers whose services have been described in these two instances had many other tasks and other clients to deal with, but each had only one client in the two cases under review. The narratives that follow illustrate, in each instance, the treatment of two or more clients instead of one, and their treatment in relation to one another.

MR. AND MRS. RUPERT YOUNG

Six years ago, the Rupert Youngs, a married couple of twenty-five and twenty with a child of less than two years, lived in a crowded western city containing many social agencies. They were referred to a district secretary of the local family welfare society. In contrast with Miss Sullivan's sole charge, the staff of this district office was responsible that year for the social treatment of more than four hundred families.*

Though the district was in the heart of a city growing rapidly, its own population was decreasing. At the time of which I write the neighborhood contained many saloons and employed casual labor chiefly.

One day a Protestant church worker tele-

* These are figures of a panic year. The secretary had at that time four assistant case workers and a dietitian, but much better case work was possible after the industrial depression receded and the yearly totals of the office had fallen, as they did before the war was over, to a little over two hundred families.

phoned that Mrs. Young was having trouble with her husband. A visitor was sent—a man—who found the family evicted for nonpayment of rent, all their furniture taken by an instalment dealer because a third of it had not been paid for, Mrs. Young and her little girl staying with her mother temporarily, and Mr. Young, badly unnerved by the after-effects of a drunken spree, sleeping at night in a stable. The visitor arranged for Mrs. Young to have a private talk with the district secretary at her office the next day, and for the husband to do the same at a later hour.

In this office interview the wife, who was three months pregnant, seemed quite unequal to meeting the crisis in her affairs. Her relatives and friends had advised her to have nothing more to do with her husband and to take court action against him. She was given every chance to tell her side of the story, and it was explained to her that the secretary wished to hear the man's side also.

When Young arrived he was in a repentant mood; he admitted the drink, admitted striking Hilda, his wife, but claimed in extenuation that

52

everybody's hand was against him and that Hilda nagged him. He agreed, in answer to questions, that he had a good wife who kept a good home, that he loved and was proud of his child, but, though acknowledging that the fundamental trouble was with himself, complained that his mother-in-law was partly to blame. He was given money with which to buy his supper and breakfast, also a letter to a doctor asking for a physical examination, and was told to report at the public non-support bureau the following morning, where Mrs. Young and the district secretary would meet him. Young, who was a Catholic, arrived with a pledge of total abstinence taken before a priest. (This was his own idea.) The program agreed upon at that conference was as follows: (1) That the husband and wife should stay apart for a while; (2) that Mrs. Young and her little girl should have a month's rest in the country; (3) that Young (reported by the doctor to be suffering from nothing but over-stimulation) should, if possible, be sent away from home for a few weeks; (4) that both should stop discussing their domestic difficulties with

53

the "in-laws" on both sides of the house or with any one save the secretary; (5) that Mrs. Young should avoid getting into arguments with her husband. This was a failing of hers.

In less than twenty-four hours, agreements (4) and (5) had both been broken by Mrs. Young, and as for Young, his mind ran along "unreasonable paths," catching on such small points as his fear that his wife would not write to him while she was in the country. He was given work at washing the office windows that day; care was taken to see that he had ample food, and a further medical examination was arranged for, this time at a mental clinic. Here hot and cold baths were recommended, with no drink, liquid diet, and tobacco in moderation. Delirium tremens was feared at first but it did not develop, and in less than two weeks the district office had secured his admission to a country home for inebriates in another state. Mrs. Young had promised that she would write nothing in her letters to him that would lead to further arguments. Soon he was cutting down pine trees on the farm of the Home and writing that he "could lick

Wilard the Champian of the World." Frequent letters to him from the district office seemed to be a necessary part of his treatment. As the effects of the alcohol wore off, it became evident that Rupert was a temperamental individual of almost childlike affectionateness, easily led, but with little stability. In other words, drink was not his only difficulty. Some who read his record a year later felt that he should have been labelled "feeble-minded," but the Mental Clinic did not make that term a part of their diagnosis, and probably it is just as well that they did not. He sent several boxes of flowers to the district office. If they were not acknowledged instantly he would be much distressed. "Howe did your mother like them," he wrote to the district secretary; "i bet she was tickled to death with them."

Two months after the troubles of the Youngs had been reported to the family society they were back in town, a good part of their furniture had been reclaimed from the dealer without further payment, a small home had been established, and Rupert was at work on a temporary job. A little later he returned to his regular employment of driving a team. The social case record of earlier days would have ended at this point with, perhaps, the following description of the home added:

Mrs. Young and [her little daughter] at home. Front room had been fixed up with some old prints, one or two runner rugs, and a few other things that made it appear homelike. The kitchen also had a strong home atmosphere. The wash tubs had been painted by Mr. Young. The dish cupboard . . . . was full of shining dishes . . . . . Mr. Young came in, it being lunch hour, carrying a load of wood on his shoulder. He showed a good deal of pride in what his wife had accomplished in the way of making the house look like home, and also in his own handiwork as a painter.

As a matter of fact, however, social treatment had only begun. A number of difficulties were yet to be overcome, some minor and some fundamental. The difference in background and in religion between the two sets of relatives—Young's were Irish-American and Catholic, while Hilda's were German-American and Protestant; the habit some of his relatives indulged in of tempting him to drink; her tendency to argue and scold—were factors to be kept in mind. A week after the home had been re-established Hilda had to be reminded that the only way to get on in married life was to overlook little things and to co-operate. At the birth of the second child Hilda would not go to a hospital nor would she have a doctor at home, preferring to make her own arrangements with a midwife. This preference was costly later, for to it may be traced the ill health that followed.

Most serious, however, was Rupert's irresponsibility in a number of small ways. He was indefinite in his statements and lax in meeting obligations, easily slipping from under them, sometimes with an untruth. When the second baby came he insisted upon staying at home for more than a week, and in consequence lost a steady job. The district secretary records:

Mr. Young has still not been to work. Makes all sorts of excuses . . . . though we were willing to see that the necessary help was provided [to care for his wife]. In his boyish, inconsequential way he tries to play up what a wonderful family man he is. He has used this illness [of his wife's] to take a little rest himself, and shows he has a long way to go yet before he has any real, keen sense of responsibility.

Of the methods used to overcome these character defects, the first was friendly talks with Rupert at frequent intervals. The district secretary's prompt service when family affairs had been at their worst gave her a strong influence over him. He was still more or less unstable as time went on, but he hated to displease her. The second method was to develop and make the most of his affection for his family and his home. He was not allowed to forget the health program mapped out for him, including the baths, but the chief reliance of the social workers interested was to keep the home in the foreground. When bickerings were uppermost, husband and wife lived only in an irritated present in which everything was wrong, but when they compared notes about their first-born, they at once began to look to the future and to agree that their little girl was not only the prettiest child in the neighborhood but that she must have the prettiest clothes and the best education. The district secretary took a snapshot picture of the child and had it enlarged and framed for her to give to her father. Meanwhile, Hilda made gains, acquiring more self-control and becoming the real head of the household. Rupert's proudest boast was that he no longer argued with his mother-in-law.

Within the last six years the Youngs have passed through two other crises without a break in their home life—the baby was killed in an accident, and for a while Hilda was in very poor health. During the first of these crises the district secretary was with them a great deal; before the second she had gone to another city to live, and, save for a visit at very long intervals, knows their affairs now only through occasional correspondence. Rupert has not always kept his pledge, but has never slipped back to the old state of demoralization. At the present writing they are holding their gains; he has steady work, and the home is now one of four rooms instead of two.

CLARA VANSCA AND HER CHILDREN

Clara Vansca kept a filthy, vermin-infested home, supported partly by begging, partly by the earnings of a drinking husband. When the family welfare society—one in an eastern city this time—first made her acquaintance ten years ago, she was sending the older of her two children, a girl of eight, to the city dump to collect iron and scraps. These she sold for drink. Three years later her husband was placed in an insane asylum where, save for one very brief interval, he has been ever since. After Vansca's commitment his wife begged more than ever, going on these expeditions after dark and usually taking the children with her. She told a pitiful story, most of it true, and always asked for work but never took any of the places offered to her. At this time all attempts to induce her to stop drinking and to aid her to care for her home and the two little girls were without avail. She seemed genuinely fond of them but they were shamefully neglected. At last, through a child-protective agency, both children were placed by the court in a Catholic institution, and their mother was induced by the family society already mentioned to go voluntarily to a convent.

It was at this point that the social case treatment of Mrs. Vansca may be said to have begun. Undertaken by A. B., the district assistant in the family society, it has been carried forward by her uninterruptedly ever since.

A. B. had discovered only one asset in the situation; namely, Mrs. Vansca's fondness for her children. Building upon this she proposed to her somewhat later the following plan: The home could be re-established provided she did her best to learn all that the Sisters at the convent tried to teach her, and provided, further, that she proved herself able later on to earn steadily in the community when free from restraint. The Sister Superior understood this plan and helped to keep it before Mrs. Vansca as a goal to strive toward. The Sister also reported to A. B. from time to time upon the personal characteristics of her charge as they were revealed in the convent day by day. Meanwhile, A. B. studied her client's background more carefully than had been possible before; and in the course of doing this made the acquaintance of a group of relatives.

Clara Vansca was born in this country; her parents had come to America from Lower Austria. The father died while she was still a little child, and her mother, placing her in an institu-

tion, had married again but had died before
Clara was grown. Clara had several brothers, all
of whom had prospered; two who had married
were found to be maintaining comfortable workmen's homes. This gave A. B. more faith in her
client's physical and social inheritance; evidently
the family came of good stock and had good
traditions. But their attitude toward this sister
had been one of impatient disapproval. By her
waywardness before her marriage and her conduct since, they felt that she had disgraced them.
As a child she had not had the influence of a
home, and later attempts to discipline her had
not been happy (one brother had whipped her
when she was well grown); later still the family
had all disowned her.

One result of A. B.'s visits to Mrs. Vansca's
people was to renew their interest in their sister.
In fact, one of the married brothers offered to
give her and her children a home as soon as she
was ready to leave the convent. But A. B. realized the long struggle ahead and did not act upon
this proposal. She felt that, with the best of in-
tentions, the brothers and their wives, lacking

the experience to deal with so difficult a problem, would be impatient with her client and perhaps spoil everything, though at a later stage in treatment their sympathy and interest could probably be utilized fully.

When, at the end of a year, A. B. had found suitable work for Mrs. Vansca outside the convent, her first care was to see that her client looked presentable and that she was in good physical condition. Her teeth were given thorough attention and the scarf that she had worn over her head habitually was replaced by a hat— a symbol, as it were, of her changed estate. Her wages were to be paid to A. B., who was to save them toward the furnishing of the new home. At the end of six more months, amid great rejoicing, the two little girls were taken out of the orphanage and the home was re-established.

The succeeding year was a difficult one for the family and for A. B. The latter arranged with the district office that, no matter where she might be, if a telephone message came from Mrs. Vansca's landlady that her tenant was drinking again, she was to be notified at once. Night or day, no matter what she was doing, she hastened to her tempted client. One night in zero weather they walked the streets together for a long time so that Mrs. Vansca might be sober enough to work the next day.

The turning point came when the sixth place of employment had to be found for this client within the year. Her work had been well done, thanks to the convent training, but some days she had come late and other days had not come at all. A. B. made it clear that failure in this sixth place would mean the loss of the children again. She must no longer borrow money from employers or fellow-workers, and she must let her wages be sent to A. B. to be expended for her benefit. This arrangement was modified on Mrs. Vansca's promise to deliver the pay envelope herself, and with a few slips she did this for several years, giving up her wages intact. The sixth employer proved forgiving and helpful. He was often in communication with A. B., and together they were able to reduce the frequency of his employe's lapses. She is still working at this same place, where she particularly enjoys the comradeship of her fellow-workers.

To return, however, to the earlier years of treatment, everything was done by A. B. to encourage the home instinct, strong in Mrs. Vansca, but overlaid for a long while by her early institutional experiences and by the unhappy outcome of her married life. She had certain half-days at home from her work, and took pleasure in teaching the children to make the embroidery which she had learned to do so well in the convent. An expert seamstress voluntarily gave the children home lessons every other week in sewing and in cutting out garments. Later, a dietitian gave both children and mother cooking lessons at home. Mrs. Vansca was encouraged to make her rooms clean and attractive, and to keep the children in excellent physical condition and well dressed. This last she dearly loved to do.

Then the relatives, who could not be given an important part earlier, were shown the wonderful improvement in mother and children. Their faith in Clara having been re-established, they were asked to see much of the children, besides being urged to exchange visits with the mother on equal terms. It was on equal terms that the family connection met in the church of which all were regular attendants. The relatives have been helpful in many ways, but a suggestion made by one of the brothers has had to be set aside. He has recently bought a farm and wants to bring Vansca home from the asylum and to have the whole Vansca family help run the place.

Close watch has had to be kept of the children's school records. Although neither is a very good student, both are at least able to help their mother prepare the itemized account of her household expenses—a task beyond her, unaided.

A. B. became so good a friend that she could talk to Mrs. Vansca freely about her occasional lapses and, when the family had to move, could say, "Remember that you are going into a new neighborhood where no one knows of your former habits. Here is an opportunity to earn every one's respect." Every one's respect became a precious possession as the children began to grow up. Rosa, the elder of the two, is a good-looking girl, and Mrs. Vansca has become more than ever a mother since the lads of the neighborhood have been paying court to her daughter. A. B. attributes the complete cessation of the mother's drinking to this new sense of responsibility. For three years she has been perfectly sober.

During Rosa's last years at school the girl did light work at service out of school hours and was taught how to spend her earnings and how to save them. When at last she had $300 in the bank, she was encouraged to look ahead and try to make it $500, though she was also encouraged to take some of the burden off of her mother's shoulders by paying for her younger sister's clothes. Mother and daughter now earn about $90 a month, over and above Rosa's board, and as soon as there are $500 in the bank, Rosa plans to begin buying a home for the three of them.

If this account seems to emphasize the material gains—the fact that Mrs. Vansca has held one part-time position for between six and seven years, the savings, the long process of teaching her to spend her earnings wisely, the prospect of buying a home, and so on—there are nevertheless other gains, some of them even more important. There have been camping experiences for Rosa, trips to the seashore for all the family, and occasional picnics. When Rosa was graduated and wore the white gown made with her own hands to the house of her admiring relatives, her mother's cup ran over. There have been spiritual gains of the greatest significance that are not so easy to illustrate. The church now holds an important place in the family life; and Mrs. Vansca, often secretive and untrustworthy in the old days, has become franker, more cheerful, more dependable. Some time ago, following an old habit, she said to A. B., "You may ask Mrs. So-and-so if what I say is not true." To which it was possible for A. B. to reply, "Never ask me to verify anything you tell me again. I trust you absolutely."

WINIFRED JONES AND HER CHILDREN

In contrast to Clara Vansca, the subject of my next illustration, Winifred Jones, a widow in her forties with five children, came of stock that had been in America for generations back. Her people had been substantial farmer folk in the Middle West who had removed later to the nearest large city, where Winifred's mother had died when she was only ten years old. After the death of her mother her home was not a happy one. The father was a narrow, exacting man, who frowned upon any recreation for his four boys and girls. Her oldest sister married early, leaving Winifred in charge of the household. Then the father married again and, resenting this change, the young housekeeper also married in her turn to get away from uncongenial surroundings, though her new home proved even more unhappy than the early one.

Thomas Jones, her husband, was a mechanic. He drank, went with other women, was mean at home in money matters, and lacked interest in the proper care and training of his children. The home became more and more disorderly, the children less obedient, and their mother more shiftless in her ways. Meanwhile, Mrs. Jones's own people, grown impatient, ceased to visit or to have anything whatever to do with her.

Whenever an added stroke of misfortune overtook the Joneses, and it often did as the years passed, some social agency—the hospital, the church mission, the family welfare society, or the society to protect children from cruelty—was called in. Each paid little or no attention to back history and much attention to the dirt and confusion amid which the dazed mother sat idle. The corner grocer assured each successive visitor that Mrs. Jones would always be the same—a point of view with which they sympathized. No active steps had been taken, however, to break up the home and to give separate care to its members. Its condition was unchanged when Jones died less than two years ago.

Too short a period has elapsed since the father's death to speak with certainty of the results achieved, but I tell the story here, though necessarily briefly, not only for the contrast it shows between the earlier and later approaches of social agencies to a puzzling situation, but because it illustrates a social worker's skill in reknitting family ties that had long been broken.

The family welfare society had cared for the Joneses throughout the father's prolonged illness in a hospital. After his death it became necessary to make some plan for the future. There were local reasons why no widow's allowance from public funds could be had. Aside from this, however, should the home be broken up as a protective measure or should the mother be encouraged to keep it together? No one had at that time any clear picture of Mrs. Jones's past—she was reticent about her relatives, and little or nothing was known about them—but the social workers who had visited the home knew that Mrs. Jones and her children often slept very late, that there were no regular meal hours, that soiled clothing accumulated, that the dishes remained unwashed, and that the children were not only running wild but were always fighting among themselves and always disrespectful to their mother. Mrs. Jones said that she had not been on the main street of her native city since her marriage twenty years before. She had no known bad habits, was fond of her children, apparently, and they of her, but when there was much to be done she would sit with her hands folded, and when some one talked with her would seem to lose the drift of the conversation at times and then with difficulty bring her mind back later to the subject in hand.

The first attempt to get behind present symptoms was not very successful. An examining specialist reported that Mrs. Jones was a moron with a mental age of eleven years and eight months, and advised that the children be removed from her care. It is not possible to be sure, but very likely this advice of the examiner was based partly upon reports by social workers of the conditions they found in the home.

As the death of Mr. Jones might influence his wife's attitude toward life for the better, and as no thorough social treatment had yet been given a fair trial, the family welfare society decided that this was no time to take the momentous step of breaking up the home and separating its members. The social case worker representing the society adopted instead and simultaneously two courses of action: first, on the assumption that not all of Mrs. Jones's trouble was congenital, a quiet search for the cause or causes of her inadequacy; second, an active program of stimulation and encouragement to discover how far each member of the family would respond to better physical conditions and more regular resources. This program demanded a deep friendly interest in their affairs, the introduction into the home of those social contacts and recreational good times from which mother and children had been so completely cut off, and, added to these other items, direct but patient suggestion which should lead, if possible, to re-education of daily habit for each member of the family. A regular weekly allowance upon which Mrs. Jones could count would not solve her or the children's troubles— the family dislocation was too serious for that— but such an allowance would be a necessary adjunct to other services on their behalf, and this was obtained from special funds.

The interest of a young man who knew a great deal about boys was enlisted at this stage. In repeated visits he found that the two Jones boys, aged twelve and ten, were "running loose," but they did not impress him as hard. The problem, he felt, was to supply them with wholesome amusements and interests and, at the same time, help them to acquire some regular habits of eat-ing, sleeping, studying, and playing. The idea of regular meal times was one that the social worker was trying at this same period to impress upon their mother. While the social worker was giving the boys occasional help with their lessons and carefully following the school reports of all the children each month, this young man visitor, for whom they developed great admiration, took them to selected movies, to the museum of natural history, to the park, and saw that the younger boy, who was naturally studious, had books he could enjoy. Country vacations were arranged for all the members of the family that year and the next.

Meanwhile, acting upon the advice of the doctor who had made the mental examination, the social worker saw that Mrs. Jones's teeth and eyes had careful attention. As she had had some difficulty in finding her way about the city, the worker accompanied her on the repeated journeys which had to be made to the dentist's, and was careful to follow up these painful occasions by some small pleasure. The health of the next to the youngest child, a little girl of eight, also needed attention. Her school record had been poor; after necessary adenoid and tonsil operations it continued so.

The history of this social treatment—necessarily voluminous and detailed, for visits were frequent and at different hours, including the evening and early morning—shows no tendency on the part of the social worker to lose patience or to push her client unduly. Pressure was steady but gentle, with frequent repetitions of each suggestion made. The attempt to help Mrs. Jones in the management of her children was especially difficult. Remembering her own childhood and the strictness of her father, she inclined to overindulgence. After one item of household management had been mastered another was brought forward, explained and re-explained by the social worker, while at the same time every nearer approach to normal conditions was noted and made much of. The emphasis of the record is upon assets throughout, not only in the case worker's dealings with the family but in her attempts to interest others in their welfare. This has been notably true in her relations with

the relatives on both sides of the house, though
for some months the only helpful one discovered
had been a brother of Mrs. Jones.

The brother was interviewed soon after the
new plans of treatment had been launched. He
had not seen or heard from his sister for years
and did not wish to see her then, feeling sure
that they would quarrel. But he at once became
interested in the new program explained to him
and offered to bear a good share of the necessary
weekly allowance. There were frequent conferences with this brother. Gradually he told
many details of Winifred's early home life which
gave the social worker a better understanding of
her drawbacks and possibilities. It came out, for
instance, that she had been studious as a child
and that the family conjecture at that time had
been that she would become a teacher.

Later, a sister of Mr. Jones was seen at her
home in a mill town. This sister's plan, made
soon after Jones died, had been to move Mrs.
Jones and her family near the mill and put the
older children at work there, including the two
school boys during vacation. This suggestion

had not been adopted, but after the social worker's visit friendly relations were re-established between the families, and this sister has also been a valuable source of information. Quite recently, other relatives have been discovered, but thus far Mrs. Jones's brother has continued to be the most useful one. As he did not seem to wish to see his sister this was not urged, but he was often given a short account of the society's plans and of the progress made, not omitting the interesting things that the young man visitor and the two boys were doing together. One day, of his own motion, he asked the social worker to take him to pay a visit to his sister. Mrs. Jones had known, of course, that he was helping her regularly, but she valued this visit even more than his assistance, for it meant the renewal of personal relations with one of her own people. It is difficult to measure an influence so subtle, but she seems to have shown a desire since then to live up to what her brother knew that she once was. His first visit was followed by many others. Soon the brother began to make suggestions of his own about the boys and the oldest girl, who was sixteen and had begun to earn by this time. The young man who had been visiting the boys was forced by change of occupation to cease any regular visits, and this uncle took his place to some extent. At Christmas time he spent Christmas Eve with the family and, as his sister phrased it, "was a real Santa Claus." After that he took several of the children separately on shopping expeditions, and when summer came, outfitted the two boys handsomely for a camping trip.

The interest of all these friends was concentrated for a while upon making the Jones's living room a possible place in which the family might have a good time in the evening and to which the children might invite their playmates. The friend of the boys had arranged for the repapering of the room, the social worker provided curtains and a few pictures, and the brother had some of his chairs re-upholstered for this new home center. Here was a point at which the children's interests and their mother's could be made one. The record reads: "Mrs. Jones admitted that her oldest boy had often asked to bring boy friends to the house in the evening, but she had never felt like

78

bothering with them. We had a talk about the pleasure of family life. She has never had the real family idea, but seems willing to begin."

So much for the program of stimulation and encouragement. But what of the causes of this mental condition?—for the social worker, in all her contacts with her client and with those who used to know her in other days, had kept this query in mind. Mrs. Jones still has her periods of absent-mindedness, her mental processes are still slow, but she has made gains in home management, in control of the children, and in general cheerfulness. The neighbors who used to be so pessimistic about the future of the Joneses have remarked upon these changes. The members of the family have all gained more affection for the home and for one another. Their renewal of contact with the world outside the home circle has contributed to this result. But a great deal still remains to be done. The need of the oldest girl for better outside interests has not been satisfactorily met, and the next to the youngest, who had the tonsil operation, must have more specialized attention than she has yet received. Mrs.

Jones can now be described as a good mother but not as a thoroughly competent one—perhaps she may never become so. As time has gone on, the social worker has come to feel that the lacks of her client are many of them accounted for by the accumulating discouragements of years of neglect and misunderstanding; in the earlier history, as it has gradually been revealed, is contained the key. The only remedy for the results of discouragement is encouragement—encouragement given with how patient a hand and how discerning an eye.

LUCIA ALLEGRI AND HER RELATIVES

Unlike the other clients of social agencies whose circumstances are described in this and the preceding chapter, Mrs. Lucia Allegri, a Sicilian, has been known for less than a year to the social worker now interested in her. It is not my purpose, therefore, to tell more of her story than is necessary to explain one episode in it which will serve to illustrate the group, as contrasted with the individual, character of some forms of social case treatment. I shall have occasion to return to the subject of group treatment in a later chapter.*

Mrs. Allegri's husband had earned good wages before his death nine years ago at his home in an American city situated on the border of one of the Great Lakes. The ease and comfort in which his wife had lived was believed by a friend of the family to have been demonstrated when she explained that, during Allegri's lifetime, Mrs. Allegri had had her own hairdresser. By contrast, the visitor from the family welfare society found her in damp, dark quarters with no food and little fire; she had to communicate with her through the only child living at home, for Mrs. Allegri spoke no English.

As this client's story, with the help of visits to her married son, to his wife's people, and to an occasional reference elsewhere, was developed by the social case worker it became two conflicting stories.

The first version was as follows: All of Mrs. Allegri's children had died early but three—a son, Paolo, who had aided his mother in every way

* See pages 138 to 143.

possible but who now had a wife and three children to care for; a daughter, Antonina, who had behaved most undutifully, and not many months before had suddenly left her excellent position as forewoman in a lace factory to marry and establish a home in a nearby town; and Teresa, aged eleven. Antonina was reported to show little interest now in her mother and young sister—in fact, none of the relatives knew her address.

The second version, developed a little later from sources outside the family, was that Mrs. Allegri had four grown children instead of two; that Paolo, no matter what his earnings or his responsibilities, had never at any time spent his money upon his own people; and that Antonina, far from shirking, had really been the mainstay of the home from her thirteenth birthday until very recently, when, to force two married brothers and a married sister to come forward, she had stopped helping regularly at the time of her marriage, though still visiting her mother every month. The older married daughter was said to live in another nearby town.

Several visits up the lake to addresses given by

different relatives for Antonina yielded no trace of her. Meanwhile, there could be no doubt that Mrs. Allegri needed continued help, and that her ignorance of American ways and of life as lived in a large city was a standing temptation to her alert, pleasure-loving, street-gadding youngest daughter Teresa. The child was found to be absent from school nearly half the time and to be going with undesirable companions. No matter who should or should not shoulder the financial burden, the present home surroundings were bad for the mother's rheumatism and worse for the child's morals. The only material assistance given, therefore, was temporary relief, pending agreement upon some better arrangement of the family affairs.

There came some confirmation of story number two when an older married daughter, Carmela, and her husband were actually found in a neighboring town. Carmela's husband was not prosperous, but he became very much interested in the social worker's description of his mother-in-law's situation and undertook to act upon a suggestion made by the worker that he call a family council at his own home upon the first convenient holiday, at which all could strive to clear up the many conflicting accounts and agree upon some plan for their mother and Teresa.

The concreteness of this idea must have appealed to the Allegri clan, for when the day arrived and the family was assembled, all were found to be there save the oldest son, who was unknown to the social worker and who had been described by his relatives as a vagabond. Antonina was there and her husband and one or two other "in-laws," but the social worker was the only outsider invited. To mark the importance of the occasion, the place had been scrubbed as for a festival and supper was served.

Mrs. Allegri was the first to arrive. Her own share in the proceedings was to sit back in the best chair, to object to every plan proposed by her family, and to rock violently throughout. Antonina, it was generally agreed, had done her share and more always, but she expressed herself as ready to bear half the expense of whatever plan was agreed upon. As the talk continued and every one had his full say, it seemed evident that she and her husband, and Carmela, their hostess, and her husband were, the responsible members òf the group. It also developed that for Mrs. Allegri to continue to live alone with her youngest daughter was impossible; that, as the mother grew more infirm, she would need the affectionate care of an adult member of her family; and that Teresa should now be supervised by the most Americanized of her relatives— by the one, that is, who could take the most intelligent interest in her schooling, her church relations, and her recreation. Mrs. Allegri's objections had to be considered and met, of course, though usually the obstacles that seemed to her insurmountable were trifles. At last it was arranged that she was to live with Carmela, the one of all her children in closest sympathy with her, and that Teresa was to go to Antonina's American home with its more modern appointments and smarter ways.

Unfortunately, this arrangement let the two sons off in a way that it should not, but the older one, who had not appeared at the conference, had always failed utterly, and Paolo had left the family meeting in anger after the truth about his backslidings came out. It was his wife's sister, in fact, who had brought Mrs. Allegri's needs to the attention of the family welfare society in the first place, and had urged the society to assume the full burden of support.

This same branch of the family had suppressed the fact of the existence of the two other married children, had concealed Antonina's whereabouts, and had induced Mrs. Allegri to confirm their various misstatements.

The rôle of the social worker at the conference had been, for the most part, that of a listener and observer. Toward the end, however, she had tried to bring the discussion to a head by pointing out the many things upon which all were agreed. The story does not end here; there have been various ups and downs since, but with the introduction of group thinking into Allegri affairs, they took a long step forward.

IV

SOCIAL CASE WORK DEFINED

THE tentative definition of social case work which I am about to attempt will have no safer basis than my personal experience supplemented by a habit of reading many social case histories. It would have been better, of course, to deduce a definition from a large number of cited instances, though such an elaborate background could still have been challenged; proof of its representative character would have been necessary.

For this merely introductory description of case work, however, I have adopted the policy of exclusion, rejecting first of all and without question all those aimless dosings of social ills by inexperienced practitioners which are called social case work but have no relation to its theory or its practice.* And for the present, at least, all short-

---

* To the social case worker who chafes under the task of protecting his profession from the indignities it now suffers at the hands of the inexpert and the self-seeking, there may

term services to individuals are excluded, such as tiding them over a temporary period of stress, helping them to find some agency or some professional skill which they know they need, giving them advice upon a question which puzzles them, and so on. All of these services have social value, of course, but, without more follow-up work and more detailed knowledge of their clients than case workers engaged in this type of work usually have, the permanent values cannot well be measured. I am reserving for consideration in a later chapter* those supplementary forms of case work which are now being utilized as adjuncts to the skill of other professions; supplementary, for instance, to medical service in hospitals and dispensaries, to mental examinations and treatments in psychiatric clinics, and to class room teaching in the elementary schools. Some medi-

be some consolation in the thought that practitioners of other professions have shared the experience. Not so many years ago a medical degree could still be bought in these United States; and well into the nineteenth century many of our states relied upon judges without legal training, while the chief justice of Rhode Island was a farmer.

* See Chapter IX.

cal social work of this adjunct type is quite as intensive as could be wished, but to the extent that many of its details are modified by medical requirements, it becomes difficult to generalize about it as social case work only, just as there would be difficulties in illustrating psychiatry in general by the work of a psychiatrist who was an officer of a court, and therefore dealt with a selected group under court supervision and statutory control. In addition to avoiding, for purposes of definition, the social work which is subsidiary, it has been equally important to avoid work which is restricted, by an arbitrary set of rules or by the nature of its support, to certain ways of proceeding. Neither "the dead hand" nor the whims of living donors nor the restrictions put upon some public expenditures should be allowed to cripple professional discovery and development.

It follows that this stage in my description is limited to skilled service in the first place, to long-term, intensive care of difficult cases in the second place, and to service rendered under relatively unhampered, independent auspices in the third place. Concentration upon this group should bring to light considerations of value to social treatment in general, for it is treatment of the intensive and long-continuing type which provides us with criticism of all our processes—with the most searching criticism, in fact, that we now have. It is easy to be pleased with the results of social service when we measure them just after the first changes for the better, or when we see them from one angle and no more. But when we dare to examine them from the point of view of life as a whole, with the permanent welfare of the individual and of society in mind, we are applying a much severer test of values.

Let me, with such a test in mind, make the broadest generalization about social case work that I can. Its theories, its aims, its best intensive practice all seem to have been converging of late years toward one central idea; namely, toward the development of personality. What does this term imply when the social worker uses it?

A Scotch metaphysician of the eighteenth century wrote, "When a man loses his estate, his health, his strength, he is still the same person

and has lost nothing of his personality." Few
social workers would agree with the italicized
portion of this sentence. Loss of social status and
health, if at the same time it revealed untapped
resources within and without, might possibly
develop a man's personality, but could hardly
leave it unchanged. In fact, such losses cripple
personality far more often than they strengthen
it. If for *personality* Thomas Reid had substituted *individuality*, few would differ from him.
Without attempting any close analysis of the
many varied and technical uses of these two
words by biologists, psychologists, and others,
there is a serviceable distinction between them
which has long been recognized and one which
ought not to be lost sight of. If we accept that
definition of individuality which limits it to "the
uniqueness of a living being, or its difference from
others of its kind and from the rest of nature,"*

---

* Century Dictionary. In the sentences immediately
following I may seem to overemphasize the width of the
separation in meaning between "individuality" and "personality" by holding the use of the former to very narrow
limits. It did not seem wise, however, in so non-technical a
discussion to introduce the third word "temperament,"

then personality is the far more inclusive term, for it signifies not only all that is native and individual to a man but all that comes to him by way of education, experience, and human intercourse. Our physical heredity, our innate qualities transmitted and unalterable are individual, but all that portion of our social heritage and our environment which we have been able in day by day living to add to individuality and make a part of ourselves is personal; and the whole becomes our personality.

In other words, it is our personality which relates us closely to our human kind; not only to the *socius* our brother, but to all the communities and institutions he has developed. There is no conflict between the idea of individual differences, about which I shall have something to say later, and this complementary idea of relatedness. Difference is as characteristic of personality as of the tone colors in an orchestra, but the differences between personalities, no two of which are alike, also resemble those of orchestral instru-

now often used by psychologists for innate make-up, but having a different connotation for the general reader.

ments in that they are attuned and related differences. While a man's individuality does not change, his personality, which includes both his native and acquired qualities, is forever changing. If it does not expand and grow from day to day by full exercise of function, it contracts and even atrophies.

When, therefore, preparatory to attempting to define social case work, I speak of the development of personality, I am using a descriptive phrase which has been assumed to belong especially, in turn, to teaching, to applied psychology, and to religion.* There can be no quarrel with

* My own approach to the subject has been by the way of social science rather than pedagogy or psychology or theology. Though I shall have to return again to this central theme of my discussion, it may be well to reproduce at this point a few brief passages written in quite different connections and each shedding some light on the use of the word personality from their various points of view.

Criticism.—"If the revelation of personality unites men, the stress upon mere individuality separates them, and there are countless poets of the day who glory in their eccentric individualism without remembering that it is only through a richly developed personality that poetry gains any universal values."—Bliss Perry, A Study of Poetry, p. 342.

Religion.—"What . . . is our statement of human

the claims of any of these, for professionally considered all are forms of teaching. Social case work is only one more form, though it has a history and a method of its own, and an approach which differs from that of these other forms. In

personality? It is no several or separate thing. Its *essentia* cannot be found in terms of distinctness. It does not, ideally or practically, signify a new, independent, centrality of being. On the contrary, it is altogether dependent and relative. It is not first self-realized in distinctness, that it may afterward, for additional perfection of enjoyment, be brought into relations. In relation and dependence lies its very *essentia*."—R. C. Moberly, D.D., Atonement and Personality, p. 253.

Psychology.—"Our personality is thus the result of what we start with and what we have lived through. It is the 'reaction mass' as a whole."—J. B. Watson, Psychology from the Standpoint of a Behaviorist, p. 420.

"Man's self or personality is the sum total of his specific experiences in so far as they represent the results of organization. Each new experience modifies our personality. It is not merely an accretion to the sum of our mental data, but it alters our attitude toward the external world and makes a permanent impression, small or great, upon our general character."—Howard C. Warren, Human Psychology, p. 384.

Pedagogy.—"The unfolding of personality is due both to inner tendency and to outer influence and agency. In part the work of nature, it is in part also the work of education and of experience. . . . So far, then, the two vital considerations both for the philosopher and for the

the illustration given in my Introduction, Miss Sullivan is a professional teacher, but one who took her pupil out of the classroom into the community and into the world. Her habitual use of social contacts as a means of developing the per-

educator are the inner potency and tendency of the individual and the nature and effect of environing reality."— Thistleton Mark, The Unfolding of Personality as the Chief Aim in Education, pp. 11 and 22.

Biology.—"Of the actual foreignness or imperfection in the environment biology as such can give no account. . . . We seem unable, from the purely biological standpoint, to give any account of progressive evolution except as the outcome of a blind struggle for existence. But for conscious personality the struggle is no longer blind: the future is foreseen and fore-ordained if only to a limited extent; and the past is remembered and acted on. This is not only so for individual persons but the traditions and ideals of a race represent its memory and foresight. From the standpoint of personality evolution takes on a new aspect, and is no longer a blind process."—J. S. Haldane, Mechanism, Life and Personality, pp. 103 and 131.

Social Science.—"Sociality and individuality are the two aspects of the one reality, which is personality. Personality is the final value, the only thing in the world worth having in itself. We do not of course mean that every kind of personality is good in itself, rather that nothing but personality can be good in itself. A society is best ordered when it best promotes the personality of its members."— R. M. MacIver, The Elements of Social Science, p. 153.

sonality of Helen Keller obliterates, I confess, all distinction between the social worker and the teacher.

But what special approach, what means consciously utilized distinguishes the service described in my second and third chapters from that of the instructor in the class room? Were those who effected better adjustments for Maria Bielowski and George Foster * called social workers because they happened to be teaching Maria and George and adjusting them to life from a center which was called a social agency instead of a school? Or were they called social workers because Maria was at one time delinquent and George at one time dependent? Neither "delinquent" nor "dependent" describes these young people in social terms. As a matter of fact, the so-called dependent, defective, and delinquent classes are not social classes, for the reason that there is within these separate groups no power of cohesion. Moreover, the specialized skill of the social case worker will be found to be, in its essentials, just as applicable to the rest of

* See Chapter II.

the world as to those who could be thus labelled. Without minimizing for a moment the importance of such questions of temporary relief, permanent support, sources of support as enter into the treatment of dependency; without ignoring such details of court and reformatory management as are related to the care of delinquents, I cannot agree that any of these considerations, relating to what might be called the machinery of different types of social work, are central to the task of the social case worker. Analysis will show that they fall into second place when problems of social relationship and of personality thrust themselves forward, as they so persistently do.

It is true that social case work has dealt and will continue to deal with questions of restoration to self-support, with matters of health and personal hygiene, as well as with the intricacies of mental hygiene, and that each of these things has a direct relation to personality. But, in so far as each is a specialty (some are specialties demanding quite other forms of professional skill), social case work will be found to be coterminous

7

with none of them, but to have, in addition to its supplementary value in these other tasks, a field all its own. That field is the development of personality through the conscious and comprehensive adjustment of social relationships, and within that field the worker is no more occupied with abnormalities in the individual than in the environment, is no more able to neglect the one than the other. The distinctive approach of the case worker, in fact, is back to the individual by way of his social environment, and wherever adjustment must be effected in this manner, individual by individual, instead of in the mass, there some form of social case work is and will continue to be needed. So long as human beings are human and their environment is the world, it is difficult to imagine a state of affairs in which both they and the world they live in will be in no need of these adjustments and readjustments of a detailed sort.

To state this in a more formal way is to arrive at my tentative definition:

Social case work consists of those processes which develop personality through adjustments con-

sciously effected, individual by individual, between men and their social environment.

What do we mean by "social environment"? The dictionary defines environment as "the aggregate of surrounding things and conditions,"* but when we put "social" in front of it, it becomes evident at once that many persons and things have been excluded and many substitutes included; the environment ceases to be environment in space merely—it widens to the horizon of man's thought, to the boundaries of his capacity for maintaining relationships, and it narrows to the exclusion of all those things which have no real influence upon his emotional, mental, and spiritual life. A physical environment frequently has its social aspects; to the extent that it has these it becomes a part of the social environment.

Turning back to the six examples here given of professional case work and comparing them with my definition, do they bear it out? Do they reveal a genuine growth in personality which has been achieved through strengthened and better

* Century Dictionary.

adjusted social relations?   In varying degrees, it seems to me that they do.

Henry James has remarked, in one of his discussions of literary craftsmanship, that relations stop nowhere, and that the problem of the artist is to draw, "by a geometry of his own the circle within which they shall happily *appear* to do so."* The relationships of each one of the clients of social agencies who are described in my illustrations extend far beyond any social worker's ken.   And, within that ken, those responsible for planning have had to make their perilous choices, have had to decide what to strive to understand and utilize, what wholly to neglect. Will it not be found, however, that a marked advance in personality has been achieved in three of the cases, that in two others good progress has been made, and that in another—the last one cited—a better adjustment has probably been effected?

But some may question whether these results were achieved by a specialized form of skill, contending that, while the service had its value, it

* Preface to Roderick Hudson, New York edition.

involved the exercise of no new technical knowledge mastered with difficulty and pursued thereafter with increasing expertness, that any intelligent person, without previous training but with tact and goodwill, could have done the same things. It may be well, therefore, to examine what processes and what types of skill were actually involved in these social treatments.

Before writing this page I tried the experiment of listing each act and policy of each social case worker responsible, in the six cases cited, for the treatment described. This gave me six long lists of items, many of which were duplicates. By combining the duplicates and trying to classify the items, I found that they fell under the two general heads of "insights" and "acts." Each of these two divided once again—insights to include "an understanding of individuality" and "an understanding of environment"; acts to include "direct action upon the mind" and "indirect action upon the mind." Thus, rephrased, my four divisions were:

A. Insight into individuality and personal characteristics

B. Insight into the resources, dangers, and
influence of the social environment

C. Direct action of mind upon mind

D. Indirect action through the social environment

As I examined the items of each list of particu-
lars carefully, it seemed to me that each item
might possibly have been thought of and carried
out by a non-specialist. But trained skill was
shown in the *combination* of these itemized acts,
which no untrained person, however intelligent,
would have achieved. The writer who strives to
be an artist in his profession and the social case
worker with similar ambitions have at least this
in common—that each is dealing with a material
which happens to be part of the warp and woof
of everyday life. The one is an artificer in words,
the other in social relations. The one must contrive to give a new stamp to counters worn
smooth by our common speech; the other must
be able to discover new meanings and possibilities
in those familiar situations in which all are
sharers, must find new stimuli in and for minds
worn dull by habit or circumstance. It takes

something more than a casual examination to bring to light in either literature or case work the originality of the new combinations effected, to realize the study and drill, the self-expression and self-effacement which lie behind the achieved result.

This handicap of the familiar must be kept in mind and allowed for in the analysis which follows, of some of the case work processes found in the six examples already given. The items are arranged under the four heads just named, and I purposely omit all details of method.

A. B.—The two types of *insight* shown—into individuality and into social environment—should be considered together, for it is only when these are combined that the personality is revealed. If the development of personality is our task, then the personality as it now is, together with the ways in which it came to be what it now is, must be discovered. The technical side of these diagnostic processes, in so far as they are social work processes and do not involve the technique of other specialties, I have discussed quite fully in another book. This side of the subject does not concern us here. But it should be understood that to acquire skill in social diagnosis takes time, though when once acquired time is saved. Failure to learn earlier the social history behind Winifred Jones's folded hands, vacant-minded ways, and neglected home was a failure in social diagnosis, with the mistake strengthened by the mental diagnosis, though possibly there was a vicious circle here and the decision of the mental examiner was shaped in part by the imperfect picture given him of social conditions. Only slowly was a clearer picture obtained, but the new social worker put in charge of the case about this time had the good sense to suspend judgment until she had more facts.*

---

* See Chapter III, pp. 72 and 80.
Addressing the family welfare workers at the Milwaukee National Conference of Social Work (Proceedings for 1921), Dr. Wm. Healy told them that, "Valuable though tests properly administered and interpreted unquestionably are, still one of the best ways to evaluate an adult's capacities is to get knowledge of him as he has been observed in his home, at his work, in his human relationships. One should always consider character tendencies or personality trends. It is very important to think of people

The question of whether Maria Bielowski's re-
pellent aspect and her thieving were due to causes
that were innate and individual or to unfavorable
environment came to the fore immediately.*
There are few harder social questions to answer
than this one.† The answer was arrived at, as it
will always have to be in similar cases, with the

from the standpoint of truthfulness, affection, sympathy,
cleanliness, promptness, responsibility, stability, etc.
Familiarize yourselves with all of these and remember
that personality trends and also frequently habits established by social training have more to do with the success
and failure of adults than anything else. They often
have much more to do with one's ability to support and
bring up children and to meet the exigencies of the world
in general than what is learned from the bare results of
mental tests."

* See Chapter II, p. 32 sq.

† Dr. Bronner, speaking of mental equipment at the New
Orleans National Conference of Social Work (Proceedings
for 1920, p. 357), said: "Practically it is often difficult to
determine what is innate personality make-up and what is
the result of environment and experience. The interplay
of the two is great and the innate make-up can scarcely be
extricated from the product of circumstances. Perhaps
from one point of view such separation is not needed or
desirable, and yet for the offering of prognoses it is sometimes essential to know just what the individual is in-
nately, and what he might be like under different circumstances."

aid of medical and mental experts; but part of the basis of decision in regard to what to do with Maria was a kind of knowledge which at present the social case worker is far better equipped to gather rapidly and accurately than the practitioner in any other profession. The analysis of Maria's home situation, of her work and school records, the discovery of the small private school as a social resource—these were things that needed to be done not in leisurely fashion as time permitted, but at once, for upon their efficient doing depended the decision of the court. The diagnostic processes did not end here; they seldom end before treatment is at an end. The probation officer was a social case worker whose service was restricted by court conditions, so she turned the task of long-continued treatment over to another case worker who later became Maria's guardian. This guardian, it should be noted, was always using her combination of imaginative sympathy and technical training to gain deeper insights into Maria's attitude toward life, and into the possibilities and dangers of the various environments in which she lived. Insight and action interplay in this fashion continually. Thus the Allegri family council, called at the suggestion of the social worker, was not only a means of discovering the attitude of the various members of the family toward one another and toward the plight of mother and child; it was also a way of arriving at a solution of some of their difficulties by giving Mrs. Allegri a more healthful and congenial home and by finding better oversight for Teresa. A social worker can be quite skilful in discovering, item by item, the facts of past and present social environment without having the insight which this worker showed in grasping, among many details, the core of the difficulty. In other words, it is possible to master a certain technique without having had originally, and without having acquired, that constructive imagination the possession of which makes technique worthwhile.

C.—The treatment items classified in my list under *direct action* begin with those services, often of the humblest sort, which tend to strengthen personal relations with a client. When Miss Sullivan dispensed with a nurse for little

Helen Keller and cared for her herself, when Maria Bielowski's guardian confessed to the rent in her own stocking, when A. B. walked the streets late at night with habit-ridden Clara Vansca, when the Young baby was killed and the district secretary was with the father and mother through all that trying time, something passed between mind and mind that made for permanence of relation and of influence. Closely allied to this eagerness to be of service are frankness of intercourse, absence of officialism, and that habit of loyally keeping faith which is emphasized in several of the accounts. Patience too—a patience born of sympathy, of trained insight and of vision—contributed much to the personal influence gradually acquired by these case workers. Examine once more the accounts of Clara Vansca, of Winifred Jones, and of Maria Bielowski, and think how easily everything could have been lost by impatience at critical moments. Note, too, how re-education of habit was achieved partly through adjustments in the environment and partly through the direct action of mind on mind, and how the policy of encouragement stands out as an important means of re-education. Sometimes there must be warning and discipline besides, as with Helen Keller at the very beginning, and as with Clara Vansca when she was about to take her sixth work place. But flexibility was shown by the worker who knew Clara—flexibility combined with no small degree of persistence, for repetition without cessation is the only way in which to make an impress upon the slow type of mind.

The policy of all others, however, which is valuable in developing the mind and social relations of a client is the policy of assuring his participation in plans for his welfare. I shall have to return to this later. Maria Bielowski's trip with her guardian to the music teacher's studio illustrates my meaning. I ask myself how I should have met that request for a loan of $50 to study voice culture by mail. Probably I should have had enough presence of mind to avoid exclaiming "Nonsense" on the spot, perhaps have thought of offering to take the circular of the correspondence school to an expert for his opinion of its merits. But what the guardian did was so much better. Not only did she seek expert advice to reinforce her unexpressed opinion, but Maria participated in every step of the process and in making the decision. Mrs. Allegri was a participator in that family council at which each spoke his mind; George Foster was induced to participate in the new adjustments found necessary in his last free home; Mrs. Rupert Young had something definite to do—to control her sharp tongue, that is—as a part of plans for the re-education of her husband. Instances multiply, but the opportunity to use this resource is often missed by the worker who is so eager to serve that she is tempted to do all the serving and all the deciding herself.

D.—Indirect action through many different parts of the social environment—through other persons, through institutions and agencies, through material things—though not the only approach of the social case worker, is more exclusively within his field than are some of the other approaches I have mentioned. "The visitor of strong personality," writes Miss Elizabeth Dutcher, "who relies on her own ability to influ-

ence her subnormal client will sooner or later lose
out; some way or other the co-operation of the
client's group must be obtained in suggesting the
same ideas that the visitor is trying to put over,
or the individual social worker's efforts will be of
no permanent value."* This warning need not
be confined to contacts with the subnormal. It
is a recurring temptation of the man or woman
with a strong will to substitute the direct approach for the indirect. But if social workers are
justified in their belief that by its very nature
personality depends in considerable part upon
healthy action and reaction between the total
social environment and the individual, then
many of life's tragedies can be traced to the attempt to make some *one* social relationship serve
for all the others. The comprehensive, many-
sided approach through the social environment
is peculiarly well adapted to the end which social
case work has in view, and it is not exceptional
to find the case worker turning for guidance or

* Paper on Possibilities of Home Supervision of Moron
Women, p. 275, in Proceedings of National Conference of
Social Work for 1921, at Milwaukee.

111

co-operation, as in the particular instances given, to physicians, psychiatrists, teachers, clergymen, public officials, and relatives, and utilizing such agencies as social settlements, vocational courses, parks and playgrounds, summer outings, foster homes, and so on.

Quite early in the diagnosis and treatment of the clients we are now considering, their social workers turned to hospitals and mental clinics for expert service on their behalf. As soon as social treatment began, such services were needed for Maria Bielowski, Rupert Young, and Winifred Jones, and they were required later for George Foster. One of the duties of the social workers interested was to see that their clients had the best possible advice about health and that they took full advantage of it.

Similarly, the schools attended by the children had to be consulted about their school records, and conferences held with their teachers, that social and educational services might be dovetailed.

The records are not so specific with regard to church attendance and religious training; there does not appear, that is, to be the same working out of a joint program, though Rupert Young and Clara Vansca were urged to attend their own church, and Clara's relations with it were strengthened both by her stay in the convent and by the careful oversight of her social worker. It is worth noting, in passing, that the Austrian Catholic church was the first place in which Clara and her relatives were once more able to meet on equal terms. A very recent entry in the case history of Winifred Jones is to the effect that a Methodist minister had been asked by the case worker to call upon the family and invite the children to join the Sunday school. The request had been made with the knowledge and consent of Mrs. Jones, who was a Methodist at one time, but who had cut herself off from this contact as from so many others.

There is often need of team play as between two or more social agencies, all legitimately interested in various members of the same family. An officer of the public non-support bureau aided the family welfare society both in making the first tentative plans for the Rupert Youngs and in putting the authority of the law behind these plans. Education for the Vanscas in careful spending was promoted by the dietitian, the cooking teacher, and the sewing teacher, while the savings bank became an aid in teaching them to save. Teresa Allegri was encouraged to attend a club at a neighboring settlement house, the Jones children and the Vanscas were given outings and entertainments in plenty, and Maria Bielowski had a good vacation every year.

Case workers are always acting as go-betweens in this way; always seeking to make intelligent use of those organized social resources of neighborhood and community which, together with advances in the science of health, have helped to make better social case work possible. This fact is responsible for some confusion of thought, and it has even been assumed that the case worker is a sort of social telephone operator whose sole duty is (figuratively speaking) to sit at the switchboard, pull out one plug and push in another. In almost any profession the practitioner who aims to do thorough work must often act as a middleman, but when it comes to defining his task we must be on our guard against substituting the part for the whole, the means for the end.

Absence in any given community of the social resources and expert services of many kinds which have so enriched case work becomes a double challenge to that community's case workers—a challenge to their ingenuity in developing possible substitutes for needed resources and a challenge to their public spirit, which should push hard to secure the community agencies still lacking, and should use, in the pushing, such effective arguments and illustrations as their case work cannot fail to yield. One relation between case work and the whole varied program of social advance has been suggested in this last sentence. There is a network of such relations, in fact, some of which I hope to describe later; for however broadly we may define case work it would be a mere fragment without the complete social work program of which it is only a part.

All of the items given thus far from my list of environmental adjustments assume no change to another and entirely different environment. It is not always enough, however, to attempt an adjustment between a client and his present surroundings; change of surroundings is also an important resource. Sometimes the change is temporary, sometimes permanent. That the environment which should have been a builder of personality can be actively anti-social instead is illustrated in George Foster's case. Here the "adjustments" of my definition, if they were to assure the desired development, had to be effected outside his own home; the boy was removed from his parents permanently. Probably the home that Maria Bielowski's stepmother maintained could not be described as anti-social but, given the cumulative misunderstandings between the two and the fact that they had separated before the case worker knew them, a permanent change for Maria seemed necessary. Rupert Young and his wife needed only a short period of separation and changed environment to bring them together in a better mood; Clara Vansca needed a longer period, followed by continuous and painstaking readjustment to the responsibilities of family life; and we have seen how skilfully Miss Sullivan used this resource of temporary change. It is easier to acquire new habits in a new place; they are not fully tested, however, until they have been successfully fitted into the social matrix of the client's original surroundings, provided a return to these surroundings is desirable or possible. This is an argument for making our adjustments more slowly, if necessary, and without removal to a new environment, as in Winifred Jones's case. In the Allegri family the elderly un-Americanized mother was returned to older and more familiar conditions, while her daughter Teresa was sent to a new home which was smartly American, though to one in which the ties of kinship were fully recognized.

Another aspect of changed environment is presented by the needs of those clients of different national and racial backgrounds in which the change had been made before they became known to the case worker and through immigration to the United States. Usually it has been assumed that adjustments in the process of

Americanization should all be made on the side of the immigrant, who is to learn our language, study our institutions, accept our ways, without any modifications in our own plans and purposes. But the case worker's attitude toward this problem is one which recognizes the need of adjustments on both sides. Even so, the social adjuster cannot succeed without sympathetic understanding of the Old World backgrounds from which his clients came. A portion of that older civilization actually emigrated when the Allegris took passage for America, and when Clara Vansca's and Maria Bielowski's parents came over.

Ties of kinship have so many implications that I must refer to them again. Let it serve at present to note that Rupert Young and his wife were more heartily agreed about their little girl than about any other one thing; it was the thought of her future and of their responsibility for it which brought and kept them together again. Clara Vansca's whole conception of a home centered around her children, and the conception grew as the two girls developed toward womanhood. In her case, the recognition of the children by her kindred and the consequent enrichment of their social background had a further bearing upon her development. This sense of belonging once more, of having a past, a present, and a future that bear some relation to one another, is best illustrated, perhaps, in Winifred Jones's history, though with her these different time aspects are not yet welded into a completely unified whole. Certainly Mrs. Jones was stirred as she had not been for many years by her brother's re-entrance into her life, and it has meant a great deal to her children in a new sense of social connections and backing. As regards the Allegris, though developments here are still very recent, it is evident that the solution must be found, if found at all, through the relatives.

This analysis of outside resources is not exhaustive. Its most serious gap is that it records no very effective use of occupational resources and of employers. Working homes were found for Maria Bielowski, one of Clara Vansca's employers was co-operative and helpful, and the employer of Winifred Jones's oldest girl was induced to keep her on during a slack time in his factory. But these few items give little idea of the varied things that case workers can do in adjusting a worker to the occupation for which he seems best fitted, in assuring better training for it, and in interesting employers in the personality problems of individual workers. This weakness in the illustrative material that I have employed is accounted for, in part at least, by the fact that these illustrations were gathered just after a period of unusual industrial prosperity. Rupert Young was earning at last accounts from $40 to $60 a week; Antonina Allegri had been earning $37 a week before her marriage. The many-sided relation of case work to the problems of industry is not indicated here, but I shall have something to say about it in another connection.

Another gap in my material could be filled by cases in which more radical changes in housing conditions had been a part of the social treatment. But here again there has been a house famine in many parts of the United States during the last few years and few people have moved who could stay in their present quarters. Rupert

Young has moved into four rooms instead of two, and the social worker has been able to get Mrs. Allegri out of the damp place which was so bad for her rheumatism; but the housing of Winifred Jones's family is not what it should be, and Clara Vansca's street could be better, though her rooms and her landlord are satisfactory. Naturally, in any aspect of family life so important as housing the case worker makes every endeavor to improve conditions.

Here we have such details of these four processes as I have been able to recognize and to name briefly. They are suggestive merely of the beginnings of a new kind of specialized skill which has for its aim the effecting of better adjustments between the individual human being and the world in which he must live. No scale has yet been devised by social workers for measuring such gains in personality as are the result of their case work. Dr. Healy suggests a few of the qualities for which social case workers should look when they gather data about individuality.*

* See footnote to p. 104.

Some of the qualities he enumerates are applicable to personality also—such as, for example, truthfulness, affection, sympathy, and responsibility. In the long run, personality must be measured by the social qualities, by loyalty to one's fellows, by courage for and interest in a game of life which is no mere game of self-seeking. But development can be measured along every step of the way toward these qualities. There is nothing static about personality—it may become weakened as our bodies do; it may be restored to health again as they often are.

I have said that any single item of service in the long list of items enumerated in this chapter might have been accomplished by an intelligent person with tact and goodwill, but that the combination of these services would have been beyond him unless he had had previous training for the task. Consider, for a moment, what that combination involved in just one of the given cases.

Maria Bielowski's probation officer had to know which facts in her probationer's past were most likely to reveal the innate make-up of the girl, and which would show the effects of environment upon her personality. She also had to know how, setting appearances aside, to get evidence bearing upon these points from relatives, teachers, and employers; and how, after discarding irrelevant testimony, to draw the correct inferences from the relevant. It was important, moreover, to find the right home for Maria to live in, since her own seemed to be the wrong one, and to induce those in charge of that home to receive her. Further, the probation officer had to report all these facts and procedures to the judge, doing this so concisely, clearly, and without bias that he would be able to arrive promptly at a just decision. Omitting all mention of the training given to Maria at the school during the next eight months, consider also what her guardian had to know about the use of medical and mental specialists, about the careful selection of working homes for a difficult girl, about co-operation with her teachers, and the discovery of suitable recreational opportunities. None of this specialized experience was any more important, however, than were the skill, insight, and patience required in dealing with the girl herself. It was necessary to know what Maria was doing without discouraging her own initiative. It was necessary to win her active participation in all plans without, however, slipping into that easy compliance with the girl's whims which would only have lost her respect. It was necessary to have an alternative plan ready promptly—a new working home, a change of occupation, a different recreational program— whenever earlier plans were no longer yielding the best results. And the combination of all these services, leading at last to marked growth in Maria's personality, constituted intensive social case work of professional grade.

In all of the six cases reviewed, sixteen people were directly concerned. Are they, unforeseen accident aside, assured of a better relation to their world, a stronger personal development because of the social case treatment they have received? Given the facts as here set down, and given the mental attitudes and external conditions of these clients when case workers first found them, has there or has there not been a degree of growth for all of them and marked development for considerably more than half of the sixteen? I do not attempt to give a categorical answer to my question. Let each one of my readers give his own.

V

HUMAN INTERDEPENDENCE

THE hero in Johan Bojer's The Face of the World—a hero whose mind had been preoccupied with systems, theories, and gospels—finally learned to say to himself, "Don't despise a single human being! He is made of the same material as mankind in general. The infinite world is mirrored in the small. You, who want to take every one with you on the way to the great dawn, help that man!" I quote this conclusion of Harold Mark's at the beginning of a chapter on the relation of the individual to society because, in any attempt to find an underlying philosophy of case work the personal side of it is so easily lost sight of. Case workers must not forget that there can be neither discovery nor advance without a spirit of devotion to the human element in which they are working.

Writing, in a personal letter, of the least hopeful and most depressing of all forms of institutional work, a social case worker in a certain almshouse said recently, "Anyone who loves books sees something in an old leather-bound copy of a half-forgotten story that is totally lacking in a nice, fresh, cloth-bound best seller, and it is a little the same way about the patients at J——. These obscure people with their lonely tragedies get a tremendous hold on every one who comes to know them." This is the spirit which destroys stratification, and when one finds some social workers advocating one type of social case work for those below what they call "the poverty line," and another and presumably higher type for those above it, the old habit of making unnecessary class distinctions seems to be reasserting itself in a strange place. The conscientious physician does not use one type of practice for the poor and another for the well-to-do. Huxley said a word which should help to set the stratifiers straight when he wrote: "I sometimes wonder whether people who talk so freely about extirpating the unfit, ever dispassionately considered their own history. Surely one must be very 'fit' indeed not to know of an occasion, or perhaps two, in one's life when it would have been only too easy to qualify for a place among the unfit."*

A reviewer of an earlier book of mine on social work was good enough to remark that its pages were "nothing if not concrete." At the risk of seeming to go to the other extreme in this book, I wish to push the definition attempted in my last chapter a few steps further by striving to relate social case work to the other conscious attempts to adjust the life of man in society. The case worker has his specialized skill, but back of that must lie a philosophy. If we would understand *what* social case work is we must realize *why* it is, and push that why beyond the accidents of civilization to its main stream of advance. If social case work has a place in the world order—not only a part today, important as that is, but a permanent part in making this world a better one to live in—what is that part and what that place?

I approach this division of my subject not in

* Huxley, Thos.: Evolution and Ethics, p. 39. (Quoted by Edwin G. Conklin in The Direction of Human Evolution.)

the most logical way perhaps, but in the way in which its significance was gradually brought home to a social worker whose interest in philosophy had to develop out of the day's work. I grew up in a world which held very romantic, "solitary horseman" views of the individual. He had been trapped into the social contract, we used to think, and should protect himself against its encroachments as best he could. I still remember the sense of shock with which I came upon the theory that society had existed before man,* and it was many years after that discovery before the concepts of modern psychology brought home to me a realization of the way in which a human being's knowledge of his very self is pieced together laboriously out of his observations of the actions and reactions of others. James Mark Baldwin was one of the first psychologists to illustrate this discovery. He says in his Social and Ethical Interpretations,

The development of the child's personality could not go on at all without the constant modification of his sense of

---

* In Prince Kropotkin's Mutual Aid, a Factor of Evolution.

himself by suggestions from others. So he himself, at every stage, is really in part someone else, even in his own thought of himself.

And in a section on social heredity, Baldwin adds:

He is born into a system of social relationships just as he is born into a certain quality of air. As he grows in body by breathing the one, so he grows in mind by absorbing the other. The influence is just as real and as tangible. . .*

Royce develops the same point of view in a number of passages, of which the following one is fairly typical:

In brief, then, I should assert here, as a matter of psychology, what I have elsewhere worked out more at length, that a child is taught to be self-conscious just as he is taught everything else, by the social order that brings him up. Could he grow up alone with lifeless nature, there is nothing to indicate that he would become as self-conscious as is now a fairly educated cat.†

Professor George M. Mead, of the University of Chicago, has advanced this position a step

---

* Baldwin, James Mark: Social and Ethical Interpretations in Mental Development, p. 30 and p. 70. New York, The Macmillan Co., 1902.

† Royce, Josiah: Studies of Good and Evil, p. 208. New York, D. Appleton and Co., 1910.

further by taking the view that society is not only the medium in which personality is developed but its source and origin. Unfortunately he has published little, and that little is not very accessible to the general reader.

This explanation of man's mental life and growth has sometimes been called the theory of the wider self. It is one of the foundation stones of social case work. We all need to get rid of whatever vestige of an idea still remains with us that a man's mind is somewhere in his head, or that it has any location in space whatever. At any given time a man's mental make-up is the sum of his natural endowment and his social experiences and contacts up to that time. Fortunately for the social case worker, the human mind is not a fixed and unalterable thing, unless it be defective or hopelessly diseased. On the contrary, it is a living, growing, changing, highly suggestible thing, capable of receiving strong impressions from without, of forming new habits, of responding to opportunity, of assimilating the good as well as the bad. "Of all animals," says Professor Hocking, "it is man in whom heredity counts for least and conscious building forces for most. Consider that his infancy is longest, his power of habit making and habit changing most marked, his susceptibility to social impressions keenest,—and it becomes clear that nature has provided in him for her own displacement. . . . Other creatures nature could largely finish: the human creature must finish himself."*

It follows that case workers can know a very important part of a client's life and can understand his difficulties and his possibilities far better when they have succeeded in getting a fairly clear picture of his social relationships—when they know, for example, the attitude of his home folks, cronies, shop-mates, political associates, church associates toward him and his toward them; when they know, moreover, his relation to his work, his recreation, his neighborhood or community institutions, and to his country.

When I happened to tell a single incident from the story of Maria Bielowski† in a classroom, one

* Hocking, William Ernest: Human Nature and Its Remaking, pp. 9–10. New Haven, Yale University Press, 1918.

† See Chapter II.

of my auditors afterwards ventured the opinion that Maria's guardian must be a psychiatrist, while another asked whether she was not a teacher. Still another might well have asked whether she was not a physician or a public health nurse, for as a matter of fact social case work and each of these other professions occupies not only its own special field but a wide space of ground in common. That each has its own task, however, is illustrated by the psychiatrist and the social worker. Beginning near the center of a problem of diseased personality, the psychiatrist bores in and in, while the social worker's sphere of action radiates outward along all the lines of a client's social relations. Where a maladjustment proves to be predominantly individual and mental, one form of skill is needed; where it is predominantly environmental and social the other; while both are probably indispensable where there is a disturbed personality in an unfavorable and complicated social situation.

The particular approach by way of man's social relations, though no substitute for that of any of the other professions just named, becomes increasingly indispensable as the character of human evolution changes from the predominantly physical and individual to the social. There is no such thing as a "self-made man," and the phrase, once so popular, has fallen into disuse. It may happen to any one of us at any time and has already happened to every one of us more than once, to fall out of adjustment with our world through some failure to meet our opportunities, some temporary shock from without, or through irreparable loss. The more complicated the mechanism of society and the more highly organized the individual, the more delicate, under any of these circumstances, does the task of readjustment become.

A sense of frustration cannot be overcome by cheerful and vague general advice. For this type of social treatment it is necessary for a worker to learn the art of discovering the major interests of the individual, and of utilizing them to reknit a broken connection or to supply a motive lacking before. To illustrate:

A former student of mine, working in a part of the country where organized medical-social work was unknown, found herself often called upon, as secretary of the family welfare society of the town, to help the local physicians in pellagra cases. As soon as these doctors discovered what her social case work skill could accomplish, they began to seek her aid in cases which were uncomplicated by economic need or family maladjustment. At one stage of this disease the patient suffers from a horrible depression of spirits. Aggressive cheerfulness in the nurse or caretaker only increases the depression, whereas one who knows how to fill in the social backgrounds and foregrounds of the patient's past can often find in them some interest to be revived, some taste to be cultivated, and can thus supply the one thing which makes life seem worth living.

Two college mates of my acquaintance became, after their graduation years ago, volunteer assistants in the family social work societies of their separate cities. One of them made the acquaintance, in the course of her work, of a deserted wife and her three small children. The home conditions were pitiable, and she set to work at once to improve the health and material welfare of the family, while seeking to discover at the same time the whereabouts of the missing husband and father. He was found in the city in which her classmate lived. Accordingly, this college friend was asked to make his acquaintance. He had travelled there in search of work, had found it, and had gradually drifted into ignoring his absent family altogether, spending his money instead upon his own pleasures.

These two earnest women began to devise various plans to bring him back to a sense of his responsibilities,

135

with such happy results at last that not only was the family permanently reunited but more prosperous than it had ever been before. When, long after, I asked the second volunteer what, in her opinion, had been the secret of success in this particular social venture, she replied, "I attribute its beginnings, at least, to the fact that I discovered the man's one serious interest in life and was able to build on that. He was ardently devoted to his trade-union and, when he found that I too was a unionist and knew a good deal about the details of the movement, we had a common meeting ground. It was in this way that he became increasingly willing to attend to what I had to say about his children and their future."

In other words, a genuine interest in any serious or any wholesome thing has within it the latent power of radiation, of making connection, that is, with other interests of equal or greater value, provided we are at all skilful in clearing a pathway along which the separate ideas can meet and join.

When I have to sit in conference where such cases of social maladjustment as the one last described are under current discussion, I am always grateful to the reporter of the particular situation when he does not confine himself too closely to the bald statement of the immediate difficulty in which his client finds himself. The way out, when one is found, is more likely to come from consideration of the nearest approach to normal living in the past, or from a realization of what the client's genuine interests are and what past experiences have molded him for better or for worse. Unfortunately, many decisions, involving the whole future of a client in some cases—decisions about physical care, mental health, vocational training, change of occupation, and so on—are still made without any such sense of the value and significance of background, of natural interests and natural ties. Here is the client and here the person in a position to make decisions and plans. The assumption is that the situation presented involves one person or one family on a desert island, whereas each of us is surrounded by a network of relationships—some no longer actively operating, some now active but easily disarranged or destroyed by careless interference, others certain to remain active no matter what decision is made.

In making any decision affecting the welfare of another (and such decisions will have to be made under any social order yet conceived of) the desert island theory of responsibility to our fellows is no longer a tenable theory, no longer tenable in the extreme instance even of the foundling on the doorstep; he too, by the mere fact of his existence, bears witness to human relations which the responsible members of society cannot ignore.

In earlier days, when social case treatment may be said to have had only one dimension, there was just the case worker and his client, and in theory at least, the client, save for the social agency then dealing with him, was assumed to be utterly resourceless. Then the social worker looked abroad somewhat and tried to master a routine of seeing, one by one, his client's relatives, teachers, employers, and others who knew him, with a view to getting their experiences with the client and possibly their assistance in his treatment. This further stage may be said to have added a second dimension to case work. No longer was it linear only; it had breadth. But the fact that social relationships are dynamic suggests that the next stage of development is to bring the client and those to whom he is socially related together, or to bring him in contact with some of these associates at least, and then to observe the relationship "in being," instead of merely gathering a report of it at second hand. These observations should be made, of course, in order to be acted upon. In some places the study and use of actual group reactions are already giving case work this third dimension. The Allegri family council described in Chapter III is a case in point. The interviews one by one with different relatives and friends prepared the way for this council, but only after all had been brought together in one place and had actually participated in deciding upon a plan did it assume proportions and solidity.

Years ago an English colony of button makers settled in a New England city. One of the men in the colony, himself the son of a button maker, had several sons of his own who entered the same trade. One of these sons, the subject of the present illustration, married the daughter of a button maker, and her brothers had established a button factory. This married couple had six children, all of them delicate and some with serious physical handicaps. The particular branch of the industry with which the whole family connection was so closely identified had long periods of irregular work; the conditions of the work in the past, moreover, had often been unwholesome.

Without attempting to unravel in this short summary that interplay of cause and effect which is so characteristic of social as distinguished from natural phenomena, it must suffice to record here that the man took to drink, and that, in milder fashion, his wife did the same. Their relatives became estranged from them and their home miserable. It was at this stage that a social case worker found them. She was still able to recognize, beneath the dirt and squalor, marks of refinement. Soon it was discovered, by physical examination, that the man had tuberculosis, but go to a sanatorium he would not. He and his wife were induced to take a journey of inspection to the sanatorium with the social worker, but still he resisted. Then inquiry was made quietly as to which one of his shopmates had the most influence over him. This fellow-workman was induced to intervene and actually accomplished the desired result.

Arrangements were then made to keep the home together and improve its living conditions during the man's absence. The varied details of this part of the social worker's program do not concern us here. But it should be noted that relatives living in several states were all seen, the intercourse broken off years before was renewed, and each relative, as well as the family's church, became an active participator in the new plans.

Details of the button business appear and reappear throughout this record. After the head of the family had been away a few months, the brother-in-law manufacturer, who formerly had had no interest in his sister's husband, offered the man a chance to do less exacting work at fairly good pay. In great excitement the wife had written to her husband, forwarding this offer and urging him to come home at once. But *after* writing she sought out the case worker and told her what she had done. Then followed telegrams to the head of the sanatorium, for the patient was not yet cured, and it was most important that he should remain where he was. An understanding was next arrived at with the prospective employer—the brother-in-law—that the same work would be offered a few months later, and the case worker was authorized to dispatch a second message to the sanatorium stating that, for the present, the place had been filled.

Meanwhile the question of the health of the children had been taken vigorously in hand. Several were found to be pre-tubercular and one to have first-stage tuberculosis. For the latter, long-term treatment in a country place was provided; for the former, a period of observation in a state institution. Another child had home care for a serious eye condition. It was no small task to repair the neglect of years, and the youngest child, a baby, did not survive its second summer. The other children are all in excellent condition now. When the father returned cured and able to do a full day's work, he found a real home awaiting him.

In addition to the social agencies, four groups had participated in this improvement. As all knew just how the change was accomplished and all were likely to be in continuous relation with the family, it is improbable that the services of a social worker will be needed again. To use the expression of the social worker who is responsible for this result, the relatives, the family's church, the man's fellow-employes, and his employer have all "learned the game." The family have learned it too.

Case work of this intensive sort takes time and skill, but, building as it does upon the social relations of a whole group, it has a permanence and a social significance that more than justify the effort. As practical guides in such work, the social psychologists have thus far been of very little help. Perhaps one reason for this is that the social psychologists have been dealing chiefly with mass reactions, and of these accurate observation and reporting is almost impossible. For the most part, therefore, they have taken refuge in the discussion of abstractions. One bases his thesis upon a single instinct, another attempts to classify the instincts, others study the psychology of crowds.* Why not reverse the process and begin the study of social psychology

* Walter Lippmann in *The New Republic* for December 15, 1920, says, ". . . one can safely assert that no collective psychology will go far or go deep which starts from the group as a whole rather than from the disposition of individuals to form groups." See also references to Professor Dewey's criticisms of present day social psychology in American Journal of Sociology, Vol. XXVI, p. 454.

with the smallest social groupings into which men have formed themselves? The laboratory method could not be used, but the method of trained and accurate observation remains; and an extension of the present case work method, still far from perfect it is true, but yet having a technique which is steadily advancing, would supply the social psychologist who approached his subject by way of the small group with a supplementary tool ready to his hand.

We are all familiar with the kind of sixth sense of neighborhood standards and backgrounds which we are accustomed to find developed in the residents of a good social settlement. Between this and the careful case work analysis of individual situations there is a field, almost unexplored as yet, which might profitably engage more of the social psychologist's attention. With feet still upon solid earth, he might then extend his researches to those larger groups which have been developed by genuine integration from the smaller ones. But for the present, at least, should not more time be devoted to the study of the normal reactions of groups of two or three or more, under conditions which make expert observation possible?

VI

INDIVIDUAL DIFFERENCES

I HAVE said that the central aim of social case work is the maintenance and development of personality, and that it shares this purpose with a number of other forms of service. But the fields of education, medicine, psychiatry, religion, and social case work are not identical; that each of these disciplines can and should learn from the others does not establish identity either of method or of achievement. Civilization will advance farther with less breakage by the way if it does not put too many of its eggs in one basket; if it encourages the teacher, physician, minister, social worker, each to do what each knows best how to do.

We have seen that the approach of the social case worker to his task is by way of the study and better adjustment of man's social relations. Every such relation has two poles, one in the mind of the case worker's client and the other in his environment—in the minds, that is, of other beings or groups of beings with whom he is in relation. No one can draw a straight line and place with definiteness upon one side of it a man's inherited traits, and upon the other those of his characteristics which are the result of environment. Life is not so simple as all that. But the social worker, deeply concerned as he is with the group relations of which I have just been writing, must not ignore the other aspect. His client's native endowment, his capacity, his personal handicaps and idiosyncrasies, the special ways in which he differs from other human beings—these things influence, in turn, the social environment by and through which he himself is to be influenced.

"It is not insignificant," says Miss Follett, "that a marked increase in the appreciation of social values has gone hand in hand with a growing recognition of the individual."* And the dual nature of the case worker's task is suggested in the statement already quoted from Professor

* Follett, M. P.: The New State, p. 162. New York, Longmans, Green and Co., 1918.

MacIver that sociality and individuality are the two aspects of one reality.*

This brings us to the subject of heredity versus environment. I must leave the philosophers here and seek the guidance of biologists and eugenists on the one hand and of psychologists and sociologists on the other. One of the best authorities in the former group states the situation as follows:

It is plain that environment and education play a greater part in the development of man than in that of other animals, whereas heredity plays the same part; but it is difficult if not impossible to determine the relative importance of these three factors. In the field of intellect and morals most persons are inclined to place greater weight upon the extrinsic than upon the intrinsic factors, but this opinion is not based upon demonstrable evidence. So far as organisms below man are concerned there is general agreement that heredity is the most important factor, and this opinion is held also for man by those who have made a thorough study of heredity.†

But our practical difficulty is that those who have made a thorough study of heredity have seldom made an equally thorough study of the

* See footnote, p. 95.

† Conklin, Edwin Grant: Heredity and Environment, pp. 366–67. Princeton, Princeton University Press, 1916.

mental and social life of man. In fact, the more one reads on both sides of this subject the more evident it is that the relative importance of heredity and environment as factors in human welfare is still an unsettled question. Dr. Myerson, in his study of patients at the Taunton (Mass.) State Hospital for the insane, suggests that the laws of Mendel do not apply to human inheritance for the reason that such conditions of inbreeding as were carefully observed in the Mendelian experiments do not prevail among human beings. "The laws of Mendel," he explains, "have not been shown to apply for any single normal human character of simple type, except perhaps eye color."* It is only upon physical heredity, moreover, that the eugenists speak with authority; social inheritance, with which physical inheritance is often confused, is a quite different thing.

Graham Wallas gives us some illuminating pages upon the latter in his new book, Our Social

* Myerson, A.: "Psychiatric Family Studies," *The American Journal of Insanity*, Vol. LXXIII, p. 360. Baltimore, The Johns Hopkins Press, 1917.

Heritage. Social inheritance belongs not to man alone but to any animal species in which the young remain a comparatively long time with their parents. Thus fishes and some insects have no social heritage, whereas birds, which are longer-lived than certain other species and remain with their parents a longer time, do have it. What this social heritage means as a factor in survival is interestingly set forth in Wallas's introductory chapter.* The effects upon man of this great body of social tradition, so potent in habit formation, have not the unalterable character of traits transmitted through the germ plasm. It is an inheritance, however, in the sense that man is born into it, and, in addition to this inheritance, all the environmental effects of education, religion, government, and social intercourse upon the life of the freely moving and participating individual, are still to be reckoned with. The outlook is not so gloomy as some eugenists would have us believe, when they advocate the abolition of social work activities and the turning over of

* Wallas, Graham: Our Social Heritage, pp. 14–23. New Haven, Yale University Press, 1921.

moneys thus saved for the prosecution of further eugenic research.

At the same time, the fundamental message of the eugenists is not one to be ignored. Social workers have the great fact of ineradicable individual differences in human beings to face. Democracy must face it, education must never lose sight of it. The assertion that folks are different seems the veriest truism, for not only have we their inherited and unchangeable differences to reckon with, but to these are added all the dissimilarities which result from varying social experience and varying responses to the same experience. Nevertheless, there are few obvious truths more habitually neglected by statesmen, by public administrators, by the man on the street, and even, I regret to say, by the rank and file of social workers themselves. The correlative truth of man's common nature is the one still emphasized and rightly so, where only mass action and mass treatment can achieve the desired result.

Our first vigorous reactions against the autocratic state led us to insist not only upon equality among men but upon their resemblances and even upon their uniformity. Equality, as Felix Adler has noted, comes to be

mistakenly taken to mean likeness in the sense of sameness, not in the sense of that fundamental likeness on the background of which the desirable unlikenesses stand forth. . . . The differences are to be stressed; they are the coruscating points in the spiritual life of mankind. That every man is the equal of his fellows means that he has the same right as each of the others to become unlike the others, to acquire a distinct personality, to contribute his one peculiar ray to the white light of the spiritual life.*

As a matter of fact there is more than a trace of autocracy left in our traditional public policy of the "same thing for everybody." I called attention to its autocratic trend in an address before the National Conference of Social Work in 1915.† Three years later, Gertrude Vaile carried the idea further before the same body‡ in a paper on "The Contribution of Social Case Work to Democ-

---

* Adler, Felix: An Ethical Philosophy of Life, p. 142 sq. New York, D. Appleton and Co., 1918.

† Then the National Conference of Charities. See Proceedings for 1915, "The Social Case Worker in a Changing World," p. 43.

‡ Proceedings for 1918, p. 263.

racy," maintaining that equal right to opportunity was what our forefathers meant when they declared that "All men were created equal." In evidence, she quoted that pregnant saying of Plato's that the essence of equality lies in treating unequal things unequally.* If we are agreed that the state exists for the highest good of its members, we must also agree that there is no lesson democracy needs to take more to heart today than this lesson in sound administration; namely, *Treat unequal things unequally.*

I have sometimes illustrated the popular habit of assuming differences and of ignoring them at one and the same time by the way in which our minds tend to act when confronted with the problems of an unfamiliar group of people—a group of Chinamen, for example. Our temptation is to assume their lack of any broadly human resemblances to ourselves; to treat them as a class apart, and then to ignore altogether the varia-

---

* Miss Vaile used, and so do I, Dr. Henry Van Dyke's striking paraphrase of Plato's words. The passage will be found in Book VI of the Laws, pp. 273-74 of Jowett's translation, edition of 1871.

tions within the membership of the group itself. To our unaccustomed eyes these Orientals look alike and seem alike, and we are betrayed by our ignorance into treating them alike. Any honest sharing of reality with them would bring out immediately their individual differences, for with each examination into the details of their lives, social stratifications would be washed away and the infinite diversity of gifts, of characteristics, become apparent. Only after such a plunge has been made repeatedly, however, do we arrive at an even profounder truth; only then do we begin to realize in any complete sense the fundamental likenesses of our human kind in their primary relations and experiences—in their struggles and mistakes, their need of guidance, their right to opportunity, to fuller development, to diversity.

During the first year of federal woman's suffrage, a determined effort was made to break down the legal safeguards which social work had gradually thrown around the conditions of women's industrial employment. In the name of an equality which meant no more than uniformity, many well-intentioned women sought the abolition of all this protective legislation. Plato's formula was never more applicable. Never had it been more important for the sake of both the race and the individual to treat unequal things unequally.

It is encouraging to find a seasoned radical like Graham Wallas urging the full recognition of individual differences upon democracy. In the field of education he imagines the teacher asking himself whether he shall treat all his pupils alike or base his treatment of them on their differences, and says in this connection,

No perfectly simple answer to this question will be possible until our powers of psychological testing are increased, and until social equality has sufficiently advanced to make the differences at any moment between children depend much more than they do at present upon "nature," and much less upon the "nurture" of rich and poor, or of educated and uneducated homes. But, broadly speaking, I am convinced that social progress already lies on the line of recognized difference.*

Here are suggested the two sides of a genuinely democratic program: It equalizes opportunity by intelligent mass action; it recognizes diver-

* Our Social Heritage, p. 98.

sity by establishing forms of public administration which do different things for and with different people at every turn.

In its gradual unfolding, case work method has followed very closely the stages that have just been described. In the past it has assumed at once the absence of universal traits in a human group and the presence there of a rigid group uniformity. It has treated unequal things equally. We have only to name a few of the familiar classifications—the unemployed, family deserters, recent immigrants, and so on—to realize that this habit still persists and to recognize its dangers. Necessary as a starting point, the classification must not be transformed into a goal. Some of the follies lately committed in the name of Americanization are directly traceable to the practice of thinking of all immigrants as essentially alike and to be treated alike.

Similarly, the beginning of wisdom in dealing with the problems of unemployed men, as distinguished from the problems of changing economic and social conditions, will be the recognition that no uniform program of procedure for all within the group of unemployed can succeed, because members of the group will differ essentially even in the one characteristic of their relation to industry. Some may be skilled workers, accustomed to continuous occupation; some unskilled but usually fully employed; others casual workers; and still others, a small minority, may be unemployable.

The error of assuming that all family deserters are alike is so well refuted in another volume of this series* that I need not mention it here.

An increasingly courageous plunging beneath the surface of things by the social case workers of our own day has convinced the more progressive of them, at least, of the wonderful diversity within each possible social grouping—diversity against that background of our common nature which more and more commands their reverence and is the unifying element in a program of many details, demanding no small degree of skill for its mastery. Confronted by any omnibus term or general remedy for a social situation, their minds

---

* Colcord, Joanna C.: Broken Homes. New York, Russell Sage Foundation, 1919.

begin to seek at once for dissimilarities within the given grouping, and for corresponding modifications in the suggested social treatment. The old dead-and-alive entries of former days in social case records, such as "woman tells the same old story," are disappearing, making way in the case histories of many social agencies, though not in all, for clear and faithful pictures of well-differentiated people and situations. A former student of mine writes, "I find that social case work is a living, growing thing, just as is democracy, and that it has within itself the capacity for revolution. In fact, there can be no true democracy without it."

I had occasion some time since to look over a number of pamphlets issued more than forty years ago, when the charity organization movement was beginning to take root in America. One of the early leaders of the movement then wrote, "When we fairly settle down to the administration of charity on a judicial system, it will be seen that nearly all cases naturally distribute themselves into a few leading classes, and the application of a just law to each case would soon be obvious and easy."

The social case worker of today deals with a more varied group—his service is no longer restricted to the relatively small class of recipients of charitable relief, but even within that restricted group the "application of a just law to each" has proved, after forty years of trial and error, to be anything but obvious and easy. The fact is that people in like circumstances are never so much alike as they appear to be. Nevertheless, that mistaken generalization of years ago will be repeated many times, though in varying forms, in the years immediately ahead of us. For this reason the subject needs to be emphasized.

The problem now, however, is not so much one of demonstrating the need of differential social treatment as of developing the special social skill which it demands and of multiplying the trained minds and hands needed to make such treatment a reality. There is danger that in public departments and in many other places the task of social case work will come more rapidly than the essential skill which it requires; in which case there will be more motions—many more, and little accomplished.

Success in the particular form of endeavor known as social case work demands a high degree of sensitiveness to the unique quality in each human being. An instinctive reverence for personality, more especially for the personality least like his own, must be part of a case worker's native endowment. To set up any one pattern of excellence and require conformity to it is not his aim. It is his privilege, rather, to discover and release the unduplicated excellence in each individual—to care profoundly for the infinitely varied pattern of humanity and to strive, with an artist's striving, to develop the depth and richness of its color tones.

VII

THE BASIS OF PURPOSEFUL ACTION

PROBABLY the most important single restriction put upon social work of any kind is the delimiting fact that we cannot treat people, individually or in groups, as if they were dependent and domesticable animals without crippling them. Governments and legislatures to the contrary, it is not possible to play special Providence to any particular group of people without handicapping them cruelly. This applies not merely to the relation of the social worker to his clients, of the statesman to his constituents, it applies to social relations of every kind.* I have dwelt upon the formative power of such relations,

* In so far as social insurance applies to every one instead of to a particular group—to a group of people qualifying on the basis of destitution, for example—my argument does not hold. The gradual establishment of reasonable minimum standards for all the people is one way of equalizing opportunity without ignoring differences.

but that power can be exerted in opposite ways—it may develop personality or it may cripple it.

Consider the relation between parent and child, or teacher and pupil, or doctor and patient, or friend and friend. The first and most difficult lesson of parenthood is to acquire proper respect for the developing personality of the child. That personality is devastated, too often, by a parental affection which cannot refrain from dominating and protecting at those very points at which the growing mind should be encouraged to find its way out by conquering its own difficulty. The converse is true also. Who has not seen parents made old before their time, so padded about were they by the anxious and fussy affection of their sons and daughters? In teaching, of course, the ability to release the unique individuality of the taught keeps step with whatever is best in modern education. The genuine teacher seeks to train not disciples but observers. So with the doctor; at his best he, too, is a teacher who helps the sick to heal themselves. As between friends the same truth holds. All of which is obvious enough, save that in the service of any particularly unfortunate one we always have to remind ourselves that it is so. The intolerable character of the handicaps under which our human kind are often found to be suffering, and the realization of this intolerableness which some of the contacts of case work bring, may betray the case worker into adding one more handicap to all the rest; namely, the handicap of an unnerving pity.

Those who have done most to improve the condition of the blind and to prevent blindness, tell us that the instinctive and pitying reaction of family, friends, and general public is the greatest single handicap that the blind have to contend with. Two who have borne such witness, blind themselves, are Dr. F. J. Campbell and Sir Arthur Pearson:

When I lost my sight, I was between four and five years of age. My father said to the other members of the family, "You must do everything for him." My mother took me by the hand, led me into another room, and said, "Joseph, you can learn to work as well as the other children, and I will teach you." . . . . I love and revere the memory of that mother, who encouraged her blind boy to do his full share of the work and have his full share of the fun. To the courage and independence gained during those twelve years on a mountain farm in Tennessee I owe chiefly whatever I have accomplished in after life.*

It seemed to me that blind people had in the past been generally treated entirely in the wrong manner. Sweet kindly folk had talked to them about their affliction and the terrible difficulties that beset them. If you tell a man often enough that he is afflicted, he will become afflicted and will adopt the mental and physical attitude befitting that soul-destroying word.

. . . . When I found my sight was doomed I arrived at various decisions of greater or lesser importance, and one of the lesser ones was that I had better dispense with the services of the personal attendant who had looked after me for many years, as otherwise he would probably become a stumbling-block in the path of blind proficiency. The great secret of success in learning to be blind is to insist upon doing everything possible for oneself.†

New light is thrown upon this fundamental principle of social treatment by psychologists in the analyses of animal and human behavior. "The peculiar feature of the life of animals," says Stout, "which prevents progressive development, is the existence of instincts, which do for

* Campbell, Dr. F. J.: *Outlook for the Blind*, Vol. I, p. 99.

† Pearson, Sir Arthur: Victory over Blindness, pp. 15 and 71. New York, Doran, 1919.

them what the human being must do for himself."*

There is no compelling reason why one should refrain from becoming a special Providence to an animal (always provided one sees it through its disabilities and does not drop it in the ditch when one grows tired of being kind), but there is every reason why we cannot treat a human being in this fashion. In fact, social workers, like those who seek to serve their fellows in any other way more or less skilled, should be pretty humble-minded about their calling, for the plain truth is that what a man does for himself counts far more toward his permanent well-being than the things that are done for him.

The reason for this will be found in an examination of the way that men's minds work. The baby seems to have an equipment far less adequate to its needs than that of the kitten, the puppy or any other young animal, and his mental development is far slower. The relatively auto-

* Quoted by Mrs. Bernard Bosanquet in The Standard of Life, p. 118 (Macmillan and Company), to which book I am also indebted for some of the deductions that follow.

matic responses of the animal to outside stimuli follow well-worn paths and are what are known as instinctive responses. This means that, with the animal, mental progress is always within a circle which so circumscribes him that he is incapable of acquiring progressive and higher wants. With man there is no such circle; it is replaced by a spiral. His response is so much slower because, very early in his career, he is forced by sheer pressure of need to compare one concept with another and to deduce a third—in other words, to reason. The reasoning and the habit-forming processes lead him out of any narrow circle of instinctive responses into an ever-widening spiral of new combinations which enlarge his horizon and render him capable of communion with both the seen and the unseen. The difference between the circle and the spiral is the difference between routine and purposeful action, between the domestic animal and the pioneer discoverer.*

* As regards instincts versus habits, note, for example, this passage from Watson's Psychology from the Standpoint of a Behaviorist, p. 254 (Lippincott Company, 1919):
"No fair-minded scientific observer of instincts in man

It is true that a man can become so weighed down by unfavorable conditions—by ill-health, unfair dealing, lack of opportunity—that it is impossible for him to *want* progressively. Under these circumstances an estimate of his native

should claim that the genus homo possesses anything like the picturesque instinctive repertoire of the animal, . . . Instinct and the capacity to form habits, while related functions, are present in any animal in inverse ratio. Man excels in his habit-forming capacities. So quickly are habits formed upon the basis of whatever instinctive activity is present, that man is usually accredited with as long a list of instincts as the animals."

Or take the following passage from Arthur George Heath's The Moral and Social Significance of the Conception of Personality, p. 11 (Oxford, Clarendon Press, 1921):

"Not merely to be a self, but to have a developed consciousness of self: to realize definitely the existence of our outer world against which the self acts and reacts: to form deliberate plans in which memory serves to guide, and rational criticism to control the will; powers such as these would seem inseparable from personality, and yet it appears very doubtful whether such autonomy of interest and purpose against the surrounding world is realized in the life of any animal but man himself."

Nothing said here, however, should be interpreted to mean that a great leap was made as between man's mind and that of the other animals. The differences have come not by leaps but by a very long series of short steps.

powers or future possibilities which does not take the circumstances into account can be as unfair as a judgment on the thrift of a plant that has always been kept in the dark. Here the removal of obstacles from his path, a changing of the oppressive condition, is a most important part of advance, but an equally important part is stimulation of wants—of wants that his own exertions alone can supply.

Sympathy in the case worker must be made to breed something better than self-pity in his clients. The remark of a volunteer engaged in war service has been reported to be, "I do like the So-and-so's; they'll do anything that I tell them to do!" This is not the social worker's ideal of helpful relations. It is true that he must often use reiteration with patience and persistence in such situations as Winifred Jones's, where the level of possible participation on her part had yet to be discovered and allowed for. This is very different, however, from becoming a special Providence to one's client. The true case work attitude takes full account of man's greatest asset—the asset which distinguishes him from all other animals, in that he can acquire progressive and higher wants and they cannot. He can acquire these, the case worker realizes, only through action which is not automatic but purposeful. To step between a man and the spur to purposeful action is to do something a good deal worse to him than what we meant when we used to talk about the danger of "pauperizing" him. That term had always a materialistic slant. What we really were in danger of doing was not merely pushing him down by the careless giving of alms, but cutting him off from further social development at some one or more points. This danger has never been confined to the giving of material relief; many who have never lacked for material things as well as the destitute have been exposed to the more subtle dangers of other forms of service—to all forms, that is, which are without reverence for the recipient's own powers and latent possibilities. Nevertheless, the two errors are closely related; unwise relief-giving and unwise service can be ill distinguished in the following illustration, for example:

A stranger to me, a former teacher who had

167

become one of the visitors of a large relief society, sought my advice a few years ago about her new work. She appeared to have entered upon it in a genuine spirit of service, but had been shocked and disillusioned by what seemed to her the effect of relief upon the families she had visited. Was it true that relief was an evil always? Did it lead inevitably to the cringing, unerect attitude that she had observed? She was unable to imagine any effective future for the work with which she was identified, or to discover any good result in its present activities, other than a merely temporary material benefit.

When a concrete instance of the harm that my questioner referred to was demanded, she cited the case of a father and mother with one child, a boy of eleven. The father was so hopelessly invalided that the mother had to be at home to care for him. She had seemed a cheery, self-helpful person at first, but as time had gone on— under the influence, apparently, of the regular relief that was so much needed—she had become more and more complaining, more and more grasping and disingenuous.

Further queries revealed that this puzzled visitor, though a woman of more than ordinary thoughtfulness, had never attempted to work out with the mother whom she was helping any real plan of campaign for her family. What, I asked, were the relations between mother and child? They were affectionate and normal. What of the boy's school record? It had not been inquired into. What were the mother's own plans for the boy's future? The visitor did not know.

Note here the power of an occupational inhibition. This teacher must have known far better than I the successive steps by which a mother could be helped to help her boy in turn to become the head of the household later on and a good citizen besides; but my questioner's new task had been mistakenly labelled "relief only," and accordingly her attention had been fixed too exclusively upon making the relief adequate to the family's immediate needs. If her own estimate of her client's character was the correct one, the woman, though thrown temporarily out of adjustment by her misfortunes, was by no means socially bankrupt. On the contrary, she was the mother of a growing boy with a future before him; she was able to give affection and to command it. What she needed, after the shock and discouragement of her recent experiences, was a partnership plan—a program of *participation* would be a better description—in which she and the visitor together could share the responsibility of the successive steps to be taken, all looking toward assuring the future success of her home. In other words, what the client needed was an open window, an outlook. It seemed to me that this was what the agent of the relief society most needed too. The level of participation adapted to this client's capacity should have been discovered and a program devised to fit it.*

* I have hesitated to use the word "motivation" in this and the earlier examples of case work given in this book because the psychologists are not agreed as to its exact meaning, but here at least we have an illustration of the way in which the discovery and acceptance of a motive must precede any genuine participation by the client in the social treatment. "Motive" is defined by Baldwin and Stout as "anything whatsoever which, by influencing the will of a sensitive being, is supposed to serve as a means of determining him to act, or voluntarily to forbear to act,

As regards the mother's loss of morale: Human beings are ill-fitted to play a passive part; in every walk of life they deteriorate under it. One test of the success of any social treatment is the degree to which all the persons involved in it have been able, to the limit of their ability, to take an active part in achieving the desired result. It is perilously easy for case workers to assume a rather selfish, autocratic rôle, to occupy the center of the stage in performing acts of seeming unselfishness in which they are forcing others to do all the receiving. To contrive somehow to give that mother a new vision of her important share in mending the family fortunes, to supply her with an adequate motive (adequate to her, that is) for doing her part, puts relief in its right place—right not only in our scheme of things but in hers. For all of us it becomes a mere tool—and not the most important one at that—in the development of personality.*

upon any occasion." (See Dictionary of Philosophy and Psychology, edited by James Mark Baldwin.)

* Dr. Felix Adler, in An Ethical Philosophy of Life, describes the characteristics of egocentric philanthropy, of

It may not come amiss to add at this point a
few words about material relief, for the subject is
one upon which the public mind vibrates at present between attraction and repulsion. Relief
as largess is so hopelessly undemocratic that its
disgrace attaches to giver and to receiver—it
curses both. But at the very time that the public is feeling this most keenly, it is turning to a
wider distribution of relief—the same thing for
everybody—as a sort of left-handed substitute
for justice. In so far as this new development
puts any faith in the beneficence of relief only, it
is going to be as unsatisfactory in result as the

altruism, and finally of his own ethical philosophy which, in
a word, is "so to act as to elicit the unique personality in
others" and thereby in oneself. "Incontestably, in the
attempt to change others we are compelled to try to change
ourselves. The transformation undergone by a parent in
the attempt to educate his child is an obvious instance."
As an illustration of the typical error of altruism, he names
the wife or mother "who slaves for her husband or children,
obliterating herself, never requiring the services due her in
return and the respect for her which such services imply,
degrading herself, and thereby injuring the moral character
of those whom she pampers." Egocentric self-sacrifice is
described in a brilliant passage (p. 212 sq.) too long to be
reproduced here but well worth more than one reading by
social workers.

charity of an earlier day; relief in and of itself has no moral qualities, and least of all is it capable of achieving the quality of democracy. Its right place is a subsidiary one. If the main plan of action adopted in any given case of personal maladjustment is sound and fits the true situation—if it is based upon genuine insight, and if, moreover, the interest and co-operation of the person or persons most concerned have somehow been won—then it is possible to ignore the popular superstitions against relief and the popular superstitions in its favor. The process of understanding a client and of developing, in conference with him, a program of participation is in essence a democratic process. Patronage has no place in it, nor can the "same thing for everybody" ideal have any place.

I have long suspected that there is no such specialty in social work as the specialty of relief-giving. It can be handled generously and fearlessly so long as its administrators have a clear grasp of the principles that underlie social case treatment and are applying these in their daily work. If that work is releasing energy in channels which will develop personality in their clients, if these clients are beginning to acquire higher wants by a purposeful action which is increasingly self-directed, if they are not being forced into any one pattern but are achieving the diversity which naturally follows upon self-directed activity, and if, above all, they are becoming more closely related to the various community groups to which each naturally belongs, then we need not worry about the relief side of our program or about any other merely secondary consideration.

VIII

THE HOME

TURNING from the more abstract considerations of these other intermediate chapters, from the interdependence of men and their struggle toward self-expression and diversity, it is now time to discuss the readjustments between human beings and their social environment from a quite different angle. It has seemed worth while to take the longest view that I could of case work in its relation to future social developments, but strengthened and adjusted social relations in our own day and time are even more worthy of attention. Our own world as we find it, our own world as we can better it, is the only possible gateway to a better future. Within the small space remaining to me, therefore, I should like to pass in quick review some of the concrete forms of social case work in present use, and to consider each one in relation to certain outstanding and permanent social institutions. These are the home, the school, the workshop, the hospital, and the court—a list which could be somewhat extended. Finally, as already suggested, no description of case work, not even so brief a one, should omit some account of the interplay of all the different forms of social work with one another. This, too, must precede my summing up.

For purposes of definition it was necessary to narrow the application of the term "social case work" in Chapter IV to the long-continued and intensive care of difficult cases. Let me now broaden its use to include once more all those socially useful adjustments which are made with and for individuals, whether or not they lead directly to the development of personality. The intensive case work about which I have been writing—the type which directly concerns itself with personality in its social relations—may come to bear a separate name in time (a name of not more than one word, let us hope), but at this stage the one term is used to cover all genuinely social services for individuals dealt with one by one.

THE HOME

First, the home. What relation does case work bear to the life of the present-day family?

I have spoken before of the embarrassments which come to the case worker owing to the fact that the relationships with which his task has to deal are the warp and woof of daily life. This is especially true of family case work and of child welfare work. Every aspect is a personal matter to every citizen. One who examines current literature and the periodical and newspaper press for discussions not only of marriage and divorce, but of parental responsibility and other phases of family life, is struck by the personal note. People born into real homes and privileged to have founded real ones are likely—safe in their haven —to assume that the subject of family life is too sacred a one to be discussed. On the other hand, much of the literature of revolt against the family as now constituted bears internal evidence of the unhappy personal experiences of the individual critics. Surely the questions involved are too big, they have roots running too far back, to be settled by personal bias.

Case workers have their predispositions too, no

doubt, based largely upon the kind of home in which they grew up, but those who care most for their subject and their task learn to set predispositions aside, or at least to make allowance for them in forming a judgment. I have seldom known a thorough case worker whose views about the family, whether conservative or radical, had not been considerably modified by the contacts of his work. I recall, for example, the remark of a woman engaged in case work on the west side in New York soon after taking post-graduate work in sociology at a woman's college. "When I was in college," she explained, "I belonged to the group of extreme feminists who accepted Cicely Hamilton's views and had no use for family life; but over here on the west side I find that my theories do not fit the family situations with which I am confronted. I am coming to see that, when the world is remade, something more than the experiences of a small coterie of intellectuals will have to be taken into account."

There is an attitude toward family life and the home which is so exclusive as to banish all larger forms of social consciousness from consideration.

We have only to remember how completely, at certain periods of history, the power of the family has overridden the power of the state to understand that the interest of social workers in the institution of the home should not be in the institution for its own sake but for the sake of the individual and of society. They must learn to recognize in any given home which is in need of their services certain potential sources of strength and probable sources of weakness. To what extent is this home a product of bad social conditions which need to be remedied by mass action? Or to what extent is it markedly antisocial and a source of contagion? Are its members bound in subjection to the strongest of the family group or is each one encouraged to develop initiative? It is easier to ask these questions than to answer them; the answer was not easy in the case of George Foster's parents, probably, or in Clara Vansca's demoralized household, or in Winifred Jones's.* One difficulty is that when the clients of social workers live in families they are so accessible to visitors. Many people come

* See Chapters II and III.

and go on one social work errand or another, each one influencing to some extent the life of the family as a whole, though often doing this quite unconsciously. This difficulty is referred to in an imaginary dialogue written by a case worker, in which "Jane," a beginner in social work, replies to her friend, "the Philanthropist."

"I understand. You mean that in a few years the specialized agencies will have entirely decentralized the family—the truant officer will deal with the boy, the friendly society with the girl, the child hygienist with the child, and the baby welfare with the baby; the different nurses will have visiting days, while the industrial clinic will follow up the man. There will be psychiatric specialists for middle and old age and a budget specialist for relief. Everyone will have a different plan for the family—"

"Dear me, what a lot of specialized persons there seem to be," said the Philanthropist. There was a pause. "What are you thinking about now?" he asked.

"Oh, I was just thinking about the family," said Jane.

In all probability, Jane would have been the last person to wish to see any of these specialties abolished, but the specialists, in so far as they are dealing either with families or members of families, should know a good deal about the facts of family life and should keep this knowledge in mind in all their work. Without attempting to dogmatize, I should like to inquire what some of these facts are.

I am aware, of course, that many regard the family as an outworn social institution, incapable of further adjustment to the present needs of society. Those who lead well-protected lives scarcely realize how many "homeless" people there are in the world today—homeless in the sense that they have lost, or never had, "the background of the hearthstone." But none of the proposed substitutes for this background, in so far as they have been tried, seem to work very well. All question of legal sanctions aside, it would seem that children have a right to two parents and that they have a right to them permanently. Unless these parents are able to maintain a genuine partnership, their children suffer cruel loss. Speaking broadly, children do not prosper without fathers and mothers who love them and love one another. If this is true, then we have a certain definite goal to work toward, no matter how far the institution of marriage may now lag behind.

A colleague says that much of the disturbance in family life today is due to the struggle within the family for greater democracy. She quotes Professor Tufts, "Democracy in national life steadies as it grows older. So will democracy in family life." I heartily agree, but we must always remember that democracy in the family is not possible if either husband or wife is markedly abnormal. The marriage of the unfit will continue to perpetuate either anarchy or autocracy within the family until a way of preventing such marriage is found.

Nowhere in the field of public administration is the state treating unequal things with a blinder equality than in its enforcement of our present marriage laws—diverse it is true, but not rationally so. Thoughtful people agree that, while marriage should be made easy for all who are competent to found real homes, there should be proper safeguards against the marriage of those too young to marry, of those who are being coerced into marriage, and of those who will inevitably or even probably communicate or transmit disease or mental defect through marriage.* The social case workers of the country should not only know our present marriage laws and their lacks, but should realize the supreme importance of the way in which these laws are administered. Practical adaptation of the intent of the law to the individual circumstances will probably have to develop certain case work features in time.†

Clashes of tastes and ambitions, varying responses to sudden external change, refusal to abandon an outgrown adjustment—all these play their part in marital unhappiness. The mere lack of flexibility is a fruitful source of trouble and one which always brings to my mind George Meredith's description of a married pair:

* For necessary modifications of this too briefly expressed principle, see "The Right to Marry" by Dr. Adolf Meyer in *The Survey* for June 3, 1916.

† As an illustration of the close relation between social case work and social reform, it may be mentioned in passing that the studies made by the Russell Sage Foundation of American marriage laws and marriage law administration have grown directly out of my relations with family case work.

Lovers beneath the singing sky of May
They wandered once; clear as the dew on flowers:
But they fed not on the advancing hours:
Their hearts held cravings for the buried day.

To resist change and fail of adjustment to it is to lose everything in a human relation that is best worth keeping. There can be no permanence, that is, with the extreme of rigidity, This law of growth by modification can be misapplied, of course, in discussions of the family. Dr. Felix Adler makes a very noble application of it to the family threshold, to marriage itself, when he maintains that, instead of marrying with the full determination to have our own way more than ever, we should accept marriage as the greatest opportunity which will ever come to us to subject ourselves to modifying influences.* Education for marriage is probably the most neglected part of the whole social program of our time. As Professor Ross says, we must learn "to make the social atmosphere frosty toward foolish and frivolous ideals of marriage," and must fix

* Adler, Felix: Marriage and Divorce, p. 35 sq. New York, McClure, 1905.

sound ideals of marriage and the family "everywhere in social tradition, so that the young shall meet them at every turn."* The content of this teaching will have to be provided in part by family case work experience.

In many of the foreign families in America, especially in those best known to case workers, autocracy is a tradition. Here is an opportunity to build a bridge over which both parents and children may cross to democracy without loss of family solidarity, as, for example, in the Allegri family situation described earlier. We hardly realize the demoralization that can come to the family in America solely through the fact that foreign parents suffer the full shock of sudden change in a new environment and are unable to adapt the training of their children to New World institutions.

One case worker found her ingenuity taxed to reconcile an Italian father's social conventions with American ways of restoring a dangerously ill girl to health. An operation was needed and the hospital in which it could be performed had been found. But no entreaties moved the father,

* Ross, E. A.: Principles of Sociology, p. 590. New York, Century Co., 1920.

determined that his child should not leave her home. At last the case worker discovered that he regarded a young unmarried woman as permanently disgraced who spent a night away from the protection of the parental roof. The adaptation made was an arrangement by which father could accompany daughter to the hospital and stay there long enough to assure her restoration to health without blasting her reputation.

In this incomplete enumeration of inequalities having their origin within the home we have to reckon with that conflict of the generations which is the conflict of youth in taking on definite personal relations with the outside world—relations independent of the family. Sometimes the home nest has been so over-protected that the nestlings have never learned to fly. This is a situation now much dwelt upon by the mental hygienists. Children fail to grow up emotionally, they do not develop the power of purposeful action and are no better, on some sides, than the domesticated animals to which reference was made in the last chapter. In other words, their homes have failed, in dealing with these younger members, to reconcile the two principles of interdependence and of purposeful, independent action. It is seldom that the principles become wholly complementary in the later life of one in whose early life they have failed of reconciliation. But the other side of the picture must not be ignored. Warping may come in quite other ways, such as in lack of sensitive response to social obligations, one of which is the obligation to parents. There are few more appealing figures in imaginative literature than the widowed father of Arkady and the old parents of Bazarov in Turgenev's masterpiece, Fathers and Children. Arkady, it will be remembered, brings back from the university a scorn of his father's favorite poet, Pushkin, which he does not hesitate to reiterate, and Bazarov's mother must give him her blessing by stealth, so emancipated is he.

Of course we have to reckon with the fact that not everything which calls itself a family is one. There is such a thing as a "sham family," and the case worker must learn to make the distinction between sham and real, invidious though it seem, if he is to face his task with courage. Something more than the mere ceremony which legalizes a relation must constitute the family bond, and a sham family is one in which this something more is not only absent but lacking past all human power to restore or create. Where there are children, the test is this: Can the children of this pair, left where they are, grow up to be decent heads of families later? If this is not either probable or conceivable, then the breeding place of contagion and social disruption must be broken up, when this can be achieved legally. The breaking up will be in the interests of family life and in no sense disregardful of its claims. Probably the only people who still hold that parental rights are absolute are those who have never seen the misery and injustice which the application of this theory can manufacture. They have never learned from experience with our courts (though there has been some real improvement in them) that—right for right, justice for justice—parents still have better standing in the court than the child has.

It would seem that the preceding catalogue of difficulties to be overcome in family life almost constitutes an indictment of the family, and makes it clear that man could better get his first lessons in individuality and sociality somewhere else. But that somewhere else has not been found. One who has observed the devastating effect of the large congregate institution or of the crowded classroom upon the personality of children begins to understand somewhat better the relation of natural ties, of affection and undivided attention to the normal development of the human being, even when the attention is relatively unskilled.

If it were possible for all my readers to know the originals of the case records from which I have drawn the stories given earlier, they would realize this truth even more fully. Thus, George Foster bitterly regretted leaving each of the two free homes in which he had been placed before going to his present one. He had the normal child's passionate desire to belong to some one in particular, to have a background of his very own. The external conditions in the Winifred Jones home might well have made any one hesitate to regard it as a good home for small children, but a lively sense of the available alternatives probably influenced the case worker's decision to keep the home together as long as possible, and gave her an added reason for doing everything by which it could become a better one. There are some things that cannot be turned out at wholesale, and a man or woman who can be counted an asset to society is one of them. It is true that the school, the club, the workshop, the trade or professional organization, and organized political activities come in succession to exercise those sides of character, those needs of contact, of struggle upon equal terms with one's peers, which the family cannot supply; but the protective and benevolent instincts have their genesis in the home and, throughout life, this cradle of loyalty and of service supplies a trustworthy measure for man's other activities.

I believe that study of the published biographies of distinguished men and women would supplement and help to enrich the experience gained of home life by social workers, many of whom are likely to see it under abnormal conditions. Let me give only two examples of what I mean, the first of which is taken from the Letters of William James. It throws a suggestive light

upon that intimate mingling of successive generations which is more characteristic of the home
than of any other social institution. The letter
quoted from is the last one that William James,
then in England, wrote to his father, dangerously
ill in this country:

In that mysterious gulf of the past into which the present soon will fall and go back and back, yours is still the
central figure. All my intellectual life I derive from you;
and though we have often seemed at odds in the expression thereof, I'm sure there's a harmony somewhere, and
that our strivings will combine. What my debt to you
is goes beyond all my power of estimating,—so early,
so penetrating and so constant has been the influence. . . .
As for myself, I know what trouble I've given you at
various times through my peculiarities; and *as my own
boys grow up, I shall learn more and more of the kind of
trial you had to overcome in superintending the development
of a creature different from yourself, for whom you felt responsible.* I say this merely to show how my *sympathy*
with you is likely to grow much livelier, rather than to
fade—and not for the sake of regrets.*

My second example from biography is taken

* The Letters of William James. Edited by his son.
Vol. I, p. 219 sq. Boston, The Atlantic Monthly Press,
1920. The italics are mine.

from the Life of Pasteur. It seems to me to illustrate not only, as my first did, the bond between the generations, the continuity of family life, but to show how, through ties of affection, the widest range of cultural attainments can be held together in relations of mutual helpfulness in one small home. That home, a little tannery in the Jura, not far from the Swiss border, consisted of the two parents, their one son and two daughters. The father was of peasant stock, but had been one of Napoleon Bonaparte's soldiers. It was a great struggle to send the only boy away to school, and through the lad's intense homesickness the first such venture failed. When at last young Pasteur's studies were well under way, he contrived to carry the home folks along; then and later he was careful to see that each member of the family shared in the intellectual adventures of the student. He made careful drawings— large, that the father might see them with his failing vision—of the crystal formations which were his first important discovery. "Tell me about your studies," wrote the elder Pasteur, "about your doings at Barbet's. Do you still

attend M. Pouillet's lectures, or do you find that
one science hampers another? I should think
not; on the contrary, one should be a help to
the other." The principle of co-ordination applies not to science alone, as this shrewd tanner
in the hills, with mind keyed by affection to its
farthest reach, probably conjectured. It applies
to the family as well; unity in diversity helps.

Years after these parents had gone to their
rest, the citizens of that region made a holiday
and dedicated a bronze tablet affixed to the small
house in which Pasteur was born. He was there,
this man whose work in chemistry had revolu-
tionized the scientific thinking of Europe, and he
was deeply moved. I cannot better illustrate the
relation between the "first practical syllogism"
of father, mother, and child, and the life of the
nation or of the still larger world of thought and
feeling, than by quoting Pasteur's own words to
his old neighbors upon that occasion. He said in
part,

Oh! my father, my mother, dear departed ones, who
lived so humbly in this little house, it is to you that I
owe everything. Thy enthusiasm, my brave-hearted

mother, thou hast instilled it into me. If I have always associated the greatness of Science with the greatness of France, it is because I was impregnated with the feelings which thou hast inspired. And thou, dearest father, whose life was as hard as thy hard trade, thou hast shown to me what patience and protracted effort can accomplish. It is to thee that I owe perseverance in daily work. Not only hadst thou the qualities which go to make a useful life, but also admiration for great men and great things. To look upwards, learn to the utmost, to seek to rise ever higher, such was thy teaching. I can see thee now, after a hard day's work, reading in the evening some story of the battles in the glorious epoch of which thou wast a witness. Whilst teaching me to read, thy care was that I should learn the greatness of France.

Be ye blessed, my dear parents, for what ye have been, and may the homage done today to your little house be yours! *

* Vallery-Radot, René: The Life of Pasteur, Vol. II, p. 155. London, Constable and Co., 1911.

IX

SCHOOL—WORKSHOP—HOSPITAL— COURT

I HAPPEN to live in a city in which one of the leading issues of several successive municipal campaigns has been the financing, housing, and general administration of the school system. The local schools are charged with the education of more than 900,000 children. One of the New York newspapers devoting most attention to educational matters comments editorially: "Our educational system was planned in 1898 by authorities who studied the subject too academically. As Matthew Arnold said of the French schools, at a given hour it was certain that every child in the same grade was opening the same text to the same page and memorizing the same facts."* One can imagine the jealous guardians of our democracy laying down the law about the

* *New York Evening Post* for October 13, 1921.

importance in America of doing the same thing for everybody in the same way without fear and without favor. Gradually, of course, there have come some variations of method for the physically ailing, for the backward, for training the hands, and so on, with the result that a much larger proportion of all the children now pass on from the elementary to the secondary schools. It is still difficult, however, as Miss Abbott reports of Chicago also,* for the community to realize that the problems of the school are not wholly educational, that they are, in part, social.

Behind standard measurements, standard curricula, and imposing totals, professional conservatism has been well entrenched in many of our school systems, and it was not until 1906 that the first tentative introduction of social case work ideas was even attempted. These ideas and methods were introduced by home and school visitors, or visiting teachers, financed at first by private agencies and still fostered by them, but

* Abbott, Edith, and Breckenridge, S. P.: Truancy and Non-Attendance in the Chicago Schools, p. 227. University of Chicago Press, 1917.

now taken over in part by the school administrations. The new venture, as one educator phrases it, was an effort "to rescue the child from the children and the teachers from the school." If ever a huge problem needed to be separated into its constituent parts and each part analyzed, it was the problem of public elementary education in this country at the beginning of the twentieth century.

Even now the visiting teacher movement has made no more than an encouraging start. It is closely related, of course, to medical inspection and mental testing in the schools, to vocational guidance, and to the various other individualizing aspects of school work, but more than any of the others it occupies that strategic ground between home and school over which there is still no well used path. There are five school hours in a child's day and nineteen other hours; obviously, a valuable approach to the school child is through his social relationships in those out-of-school hours. I am indebted, for the most part, in the brief account of visiting teaching which follows, to a pamphlet recently published by the Public

Education Association of New York, which gives the results of correspondence with 60 visiting teachers in 28 cities.

A visiting teacher is a social worker, preferably one with some classroom experience of teaching. She undertakes, for a given number of pupils reported to her by the school for poor scholarship, bad health, misconduct, lateness, irregular attendance, or for what appear to be adverse home conditions, to discover the causal factors in the difficulty and then tries to work out a better adjustment. It is not astonishing to find that, among the measures she most frequently employs, are the exercising of personal influence, winning the co-operation of parents, seeking the advice and assistance of medical and mental experts, seeking the aid of the various social agencies, utilizing recreational facilities, and changing the child's environment. We have seen repeatedly that these are the measures most frequently used by all social case workers. "Change of environment" may mean a change outside any school, within the present school, or to another school. Such changes within the present school as a promotion, a demotion, and a transfer to a special class, are based on information brought back to the teachers after a study of the individual child in his neighborhood environment and in that of his home. The analysis of replies to inquiries sent out shows that

Even in schools where the children have been reclassified on the basis of mentality, visiting teachers report having found children whose scholastic attainments did not tally with their intelligence quotients, and whose "physical condition," " out-of-school influences," "family history," " character disabilities," etc., had to be taken into account in interpreting their failures. Adjustment of the adverse home conditions, whatever they were, resulted in bringing these children up in lessons to the level where their intelligence showed they should be. The following history illustrates this type of child: A boy of nine with an intelligence quotient of 120 was doing very poor work, in the 4th grade. The visiting teacher found that he read till 11 at night "any books he found in the library." He rarely went out—"not in this neighborhood!" The visiting teacher correlated his reading with his lessons; interested him in outdoor athletics; and with the mother worked out a vigorous daily program which left him at night physically tired and mentally satisfied, and ready to retire early. Interest and oversight brought this child up to the standard which his ability warranted, and in addition changed him from a dreamer and laggard into an energetic boy and pupil.*

There is one discouraging aspect of this new development in social case work. Those engaged in the task, some under public auspices and some under private, are often overburdened with more work than they can possibly do well. A visiting teacher who has to deal with more than 200 children a year is not doing social case work or very much else of a socially productive character. In many school systems the annual load for each worker is from 300 to 500, and some report a case-load of 1,000. Even the figure of 200 children is altogether too high; if the work is to yield needed insights and to make its full contribution to the remolding of school policies, it might well be cut in half. As it is, the figures submitted in the report published by the Public Education Association show that in some of the

* The Visiting Teacher in the United States, p. 33 sq. A Survey by the National Association of Visiting Teachers and Home and School Visitors. New York, Public Education Association, 1921.

28 cities replying to inquiries they have the term "visiting teaching" without the service.

No one of the organized forms of social life can be studied save against a background of all the others. Consider, for example, the network of relations existing between the home and the workshop. More than thirteen years ago, at a meeting of social workers, I ventured to take the position, then sharply challenged, that all the larger adjustments of industry, finance, international relations, government itself, could be tested in the long run by their effect upon family life; that they must conform finally to the needs of the home or else be scrapped or reorganized.* Some of my hearers felt that these other social institutions rather than the family were likely to be the winners in what seemed to them an unequal contest. But I must have failed to make my meaning clear; at least, I have seen no reason to change my mind on this point. If, for example, the railroad trainman cannot see his

* Proceedings of the National Conference of Charities and Correction (now the National Conference of Social Work) for 1908, p. 77.

children often enough really to know them and for them to know him; if it be true that long working hours, or low wages, or sudden transfers of large bodies of workmen to a distant point are destructive of a sound family life, then industry itself cannot fail to be crippled by the inevitable reaction against such social blindness, and a reorganization of industry becomes inevitable if civilization is to survive.

It is possible, of course, to turn this illustration about and demonstrate that some of the bases of family life itself had their roots in economic and labor conditions. Thus Vinogradoff, in his brief review of tribal law, shows how often both tribal organization and marital customs were shaped by the surrounding physical and industrial conditions.* The two views are not irreconcilable; one relates to origins, the other to possible future developments.

Mention of some very recently organized relations between industry and social case work may

* Vinogradoff, Sir Paul: Outlines of Historical Jurisprudence, Vol. I, pp. 163–212. Oxford University Press, 1920.

suggest what certain trends in industry now are. One of the first contacts of case work with industry came about through the child labor campaigns, but I am reserving any account of these and of some other relations with industry for a separate chapter, because they will serve to illustrate the interplay of all the types of social work in effecting certain important social reforms.

The actual entry of case work into the administrative side of industry is very recent. Changes in methods of production which account for this new departure were indicated by the late Franklin K. Lane when he wrote, at the end of his term of service in the Department of the Interior, "We are quickly passing out of the rough-and-ready period of our national life, in which we have dealt wholesale with men and things, into a period of more intensive development in which we must seek to find the special qualities of the individual unit, whether that unit be an acre of desert, a barrel of oil, a mountain canyon, the flow of a river, or the capacity of the humblest of men."

It is not possible to dwell here upon the details

of "personnel work," as it is called, but it should be evident that not only this service, as now developed in factories and workshops, but the specialized division of it which has to do with the mental hygiene of industrial workers will have to utilize the qualities and technique which belong to the social case worker.

Another interesting application of case work to industrial problems is in the workmen's compensation field. The New York State Industrial Commission has employed two trained case workers to collect the social facts which will be helpful to the Commission in making individual decisions about cases of workmen's compensation. Their services also include such tasks as selecting proper guardians (where the beneficiaries of the award are children), following up the award by some specialized service which will render the compensation more effective (securing training, work for cripples, medical service, and so on), and making connection with the social resources of the community wherever difficulties are brought to light with which the Commission cannot possibly deal. Miss Frances Perkins, to whom the state owes the inauguration of this service, gives the following illustration, among others, of its value:

The father of the Hogan family was burned to death in 1916. The mother was already dead. The Commission at that time had the children's uncle, Mr. Craig, assume the guardianship of the children and recei e the money for their support. Some time in 1920 it was noted that Mr. Craig no longer signed receipts for the money and a letter brought the response from Mrs. Craig that her husband was not home and that she was receiving the money instead. The After-Care Service was later asked to look into the case, chiefly because the Commissioner remembered the unusual beauty and charm of the Hogan children and wondered how they were getting along.

The family was found living in wretched surroundings. Mr. Craig was serving a five years' sentence for burglary. Mrs. Craig was doing work by the day and Mary Hogan was kept out of school to care for the small children. Tom Hogan, the eighteen-year-old boy, was found to be badly crippled as a result of a street accident, and much in need of medical care. It proved to be easy to secure a grant from the widow's pension fund for Mrs. Craig which, with the Hogan children's compensation and help from some of the Hogan relatives who were visited, enabled Mrs. Craig to remain at home and care for the children. Mary Hogan was sent to school, Tom was placed under the care of a good orthopædic clinic and is just recovering from an operation which will straighten the twisted leg to nearly normal. In this case our advice to the Commission was to continue payments for the children in the Craig home, but it was only after considerable work that conditions were such as to warrant this recommendation.*

Probably there are many other points involving the relation of the economically stronger to the economically weaker in which a law, however well drawn, or the usual routine of administration, however orderly, will fall short of achieving essential justice unless administration can include these case by case adjustments. But I pass on to the one other question under this general heading of the workshop that I can attempt even to mention; namely, finding work. The phrases "vocational guidance" and "vocational education" have been in every one's mouth this long while, but the actual working out of a sound technique of procedure looking to the best welfare of each individual dealt with has arrived very slowly. To this delay may be traced some

* Perkins, Frances: "An Experiment in the Application of Case Work Methods to a New Problem," in *The Family* for April, 1921.

of the serious breakdowns of our after-the-war vocational program.

The public employment bureaus of the war period, necessary as they were, had some of the same drawbacks. In theory, they had only one task: to bring together the man in need of work and the man in need of a worker. But the assumption that these two parties to a bargain meet on equal terms is not always borne out by the facts. Here, too, in time, must come the social adjustments which are already being made in some of the juvenile departments of state employment bureaus where, as one official expresses it, they are trying, in placing a young person, to take into account the applicant's special aptitudes, training, physique, home environment, and personality. After placing him, they are also careful to get some idea of the result of placement. No employment bureau can make decisions for either worker or employer, but it can strengthen the basis of decision for both by putting at the disposal of each a clearer picture of the concrete situation.

This is not the place in which to attempt a detailed account of social case work in periods of industrial depression, though the temporary care of the unemployed and their families has always been a case work burden at these times, and the fact of unemployment has been a fruitful cause of other maladjustments demanding social treatment for years after the period of depression was over. Violent fluctuations between times of great scarcity of workers and times of great scarcity of work are due to causes over which the social agencies of the country have little control. They realize this, and the very agencies that have done most to mitigate the disastrous effects of hard times are the ones that have most persistently urged preventive measures upon government and upon industry. "When people are sick," to quote from a report of mine written after the panic of 1907–08, "we can cure them; when they are bad, we can try to reform them; but when they are out of work there is only one effective remedy for their troubles and that is real work at real wages."

Certain aspects of the situation, however, will continue to need the technique of the case worker. In an earlier chapter mention was made, in passing, of the varied types of the unemployed and of the importance of differentiation in their treatment.* The more varied and flexible the measures taken by employers and by the public, the more surely will the worst evils of business cycles disappear. Meanwhile, the social agencies are far from being indifferent to the tragedy of the unemployed man or woman. Such remedial measures as they are able to take they do take, preserving intact, in so far as possible, their policy of diversified service. To quote again from the 1908 report, they "make a loan to one, send another to the woodyard to work for all he gets, stave off the landlord's eviction notice for a third, find a chance of work outside for a fourth, place the fifth in a hospital, send the sixth and his whole family to the country, provide cash for the exceptionally provident buyer who is the seventh, relieve the improvident eighth sparingly with supplies plus a work-test, and, instead of doing work twice over, turn the

*See Chapter VI, p. 154.

ninth over to the charity that is already caring
for him."

But, just as after a public disaster all disabilities are in danger of being credited to the earth-
quake, or flood, or fire, so in a time of industrial
depression social agencies are in danger of assuming that their clients are in need of nothing but
employment, when in fact their most serious maladjustments may be quite other. This blindness
of the preoccupied might have wrecked the treatment of Rupert Young and his family, as will be
explained in the next chapter.*

I have just been discussing a failure in industrial organization which periodically thrusts upon
social case work the handling of a mass problem
with which it is ill fitted to cope. In sharp contrast to this industrial breakdown is the strong
organization achieved in this generation by medicine and the hospital. Not only have the wonderful advances of medicine and surgery and
public sanitation supplied the family agencies
and those engaged in children's social work with

*See p. 239 sq.

a whole battery of new resources, but they have also developed within the hospital itself a new and most valuable adaptation of social case work to the needs of patients in the dispensary and the wards.

Social service in the hospital had its beginnings in the desire of forward-looking physicians to achieve better and more lasting results. They found that social insights strengthened their diagnosis, and social adjustments their therapy. Here, in medicine, note again the line of development to which I have called attention more than once in other connections: first, in the long, slow progress there was promiscuous dosing, then a dogmatic same-thing-for-everybody, then the more or less scientific classification of diseases and a standardized treatment for each. Now, however, socialized medicine begins to treat not only the disease but the patient in his individual environment—a marriage, as it were, of medicine and social work. Preventive medicine owes its vitality and its continuing advance not only to laboratory experimentation and new discoveries, but to the application of such discoveries to life, to the adaptations and new problems presented by the medical clinician, and by the reports of social workers upon environmental obstacles and end results.

About three hundred and fifty hospitals in the United States now have social service departments. This development has sometimes outstripped the supply of competent medical-social workers. Progress has also been delayed, in some hospitals, by the tendency to overload the social case workers with administrative duties which could be as well performed by others. But all types of social case work owe a great debt to modifications in method worked out in dispensary and hospital by the case workers there who have been doing their work under new conditions and in close co-operation with the highly skilled practitioners of another profession. The trained case worker interprets the community to the hospital and the hospital to the community. In the matter of hospital admissions and discharges, the social worker can make a whole series of adjustments that are time-saving and life-saving. At the same time, however, Miss Ida Cannon's warning should be heeded when she says:

At present, the administrative function of the social worker in the clinic is crowding out her social case work. She is too busy to get into the homes, to keep fresh and clear before her the social situation in the background. Thus she becomes an institutionalized person and loses the biggest contribution she has to give to the hospital, that of never thinking in routine, of keeping fresh always the community's and patient's point of view.*

A branch of medical-social case work which has developed quite rapidly since the war is what is known as psychiatric social work. It is only when such social work is undertaken in close collaboration with a thoroughly competent psychiatrist that it concerns us here. The value of collaboration must be apparent, since, in the mental field even more than in the physical, thorough diagnosis must depend in part upon social evidence, and the treatment which follows is so

* Cannon, Ida M.: Address before the American Hospital Association, October, 1920. See also Miss Cannon's book, Social Work in Hospitals, published by the Russell Sage Foundation.

largely a matter of better adjustment to the environment.*

Probably every one would agree that tradition and precedent are more heavily weighing down and clogging the daily procedures of courts than of hospitals. Both, however, are under the control of long-established professions, and to the extent that these professions are highly organized and class-conscious the social worker in the court or hospital is often at a certain disadvantage. It is important, therefore, for the social case worker who enters hospital or court service to be thoroughly well grounded in the principles and technique of social work in advance. "We read, indeed," says George Eliot, "that the walls of Jericho fell down before the sound of trumpets; but we nowhere hear that those trumpets were hoarse and feeble."

The court is the last of the social institutions that I can here consider, and by court I must be understood to mean the whole machinery of justice, including its functions of interpretation

* See footnote, p. 104.

and of enforcement. In the old days these functions were perverted by our blind desire to punish and to avenge. Later came the attempt to make the punishment fit the crime. Now we are only just beginning to realize that we should make the punishment (the treatment rather) fit the criminal. Dean Roscoe Pound tells us that

The nineteenth century was hostile to individualization and to administrative discretion, which is the chief agency of individualization, seeking to reduce the whole administration of justice to abstractly just, formal, rigid rules, mechanically administered. This was true the world over. It was specially true, and true to an exaggerated degree, in America. . . . Hence, we got rigid detailed procedure and hard-and-fast schemes of penal treatment, lest prosecutor or court or prison authorities do something spontaneous in view of the exigencies of a particular case.*

Modern courts are turning to certain groups of specialists no longer as expert witnesses, summoned by the prosecution and the defense to prove that black is not so black and white not so white after all, but as disinterested advisers of the court itself, serving neither side of the con-

* Pound and Frankfurter: Criminal Justice in Cleveland. Cleveland Foundation, 1922.

troversy or cause but seeking the point at which the best interests of society and of the individuals involved may be said to meet. With the gradual development of probation, of the suspended sentence and parole, and of the indeterminate sentence, there has come the opportunity of the physician, the psychologist, the psychiatrist, and of the social worker to suggest different things that should be taken into consideration in judging a man, and certain other things that may be done—different things for different people—in placing his life under the temporary guidance and control of the state.

The plan of juvenile and adult probation is probably the most important single agency through which social work now enters the courts. Juvenile probation originated with a private child-helping agency in the '60's, but even now its use by the courts is far from being thoroughly effective. In this field of fixed traditions and formal judgments changes come slowly. Thus, probation is still used in some courts as a substitute for an unpopular and difficult decision; it is still used, moreover, in cases in which probation is bound to be ineffectual.* It follows from these misapplications of a good method that conscientious probation officers are burdened with more cases than they can possibly treat effectively, and again we find a form of case work laboring under the disadvantage of unwieldy numbers. This is very far from being universally true in the probation field, where some excellent case work has been done, but it is truer than it should be. In Maria Bielowski's story is recorded the good work of a probation officer who, it will be remembered, gathered the social evidence in the case before sentence was pronounced.

The best of the lawyers and judges look forward to many changes in court procedure. When I was preparing the manuscript of a book on Social Diagnosis, I asked a well-known authority on the law of evidence to read and criticize some of my chapters. He was good enough to do this, and many of his criticisms were wholesomely

* See, for example, Bulletin 2 of the Seybert Institution of Philadelphia on the Handling of Cases by the Juvenile Court and Court of Domestic Relations in that city.

severe. But he added that he had not realized before what a rich field of usefulness there could be for evidence outside the court room. "The great thing," he continued, "is that in the court of the next generation, with its staff of social workers, these materials and methods will be the main ones, and some large part of our present technical rules will have gone by the board."

There is a long road to travel before any of us can lay claim to such a knowledge of the elements of social evidence, to such skill in effecting better adjustments between men and their social environment, as will even begin to justify this prophecy, but the goal is worth striving for, and, meanwhile, every stage of the journey is full of interest and instruction.

It must not be inferred that the home, the school, the workshop, the hospital, and the court are the only places in which social case work has already proved of service, or in which it will have to bear an important part in shaping future policies. Even in these five social institutions, only a few of the case work developments already achieved have here been indicated. Thus nothing has been said of the combination of domestic science and case work in improved household management, and nothing of the technique now well developed for that rehabilitation of homes which must follow public disasters. The protection of children from cruelty and neglect is one branch of child welfare service, while special case work with difficult children and with those placed out in foster homes form two other well defined child-helping specialties. Another field not yet developed might be the application of the principles of family and child welfare to the administration of trust estates, where financial institutions now responsible as administrators of small annuities and the like which go to minors and to maladjusted adults could incidentally serve the social as well as the material welfare of their clients.

Nothing has been said in connection with schools about the possible social developments in their attendance departments, though the attendance officer's task, rightly understood, is a social one. The issuers of working papers to school children and those who attempt vocational guidance should have some knowledge of case work technique.

Shop management, and responsibility for employing, classifying, and promoting workers involves many of these same processes. Commissions for the blind, societies for the care of cripples, agencies for the re-education of the handicapped, find social case work an important adjunct. In the prisons and reformatories of the country this way of dealing with inmates individually is not yet well established save in the exceptional institution, but at least parole officers and after-care agents should be case workers. Legal aid societies were organized by lawyers, but a number of their promoters are now seeking closer relations with family welfare societies in order to combine, in such service, the social with the legal point of view. A recent development has been the application of social case work to the better care and disposition of stranded travelers. The immigrant just arriving at an American port might be supposed to stand more in need of skilful individualized guidance than any one else.

As a matter of fact he does. But this particular responsibility has been left in unskilled hands too often or has not been discharged at all, so that there is no adequate development of case work at our national gateways today, though public attention has been called to this serious lack, and there is reason to hope that it may soon be supplied.

Every month or so, some new and beneficent application of social case work to human welfare —often from an entirely unexpected quarter— comes to my attention. Sometimes the new development is far removed from the types of service in which case work originated. One of these, for example, comes in the private practice of physicians and psychiatrists, who, after seeing what case work can do in their free clinics, are seeking the services of case workers for their well-to-do patients. How rapidly social case work will develop a private practice of its own cannot be predicted, but it should be evident from the examples given in this book that the skill here described can be utilized quite as well in the homes of the rich as in those of the poor, that, in the one as in the other, personality can be thwarted and retarded, developed and enriched.

X

THE FORMS OF SOCIAL WORK AND THEIR INTERRELATIONS

SAINTE-BEUVE tells of a surgeon in the time of Louis XIV who once said to Chancellor Daguesseau that he wished to see an impassable wall of separation erected between surgery and medicine. The Chancellor replied, "But, monsieur, on which side of the wall will you place the patient?" The Chancellor's question is still a pertinent one in most professions. Everywhere the specialist is in danger of developing an insular habit of mind, and the phenomenon does occur occasionally even within the boundaries of social work. We have seen that a certain specialized form of skill has been taken by the social case worker into our homes, courts, schools, medical institutions, and industries. But quite as important as this skill and quite as much needed in these institutions is the case worker's sense of the whole of social work and of the relation of each part to that whole.

The other forms of social work, all of which interplay with case work, are three—group work, social reform, and social research. Case work seeks to effect better social relations by dealing with individuals one by one or within the intimate group of the family. But social work also achieves the same general ends in these other ways. It includes a wide variety of group activities—settlement work, recreational work, club, neighborhood and local community work—in which the individual, though still met face to face, becomes one of a number. By a method different from that employed in either case or group work, though with the same end in view, social reform seeks to improve conditions in the mass, chiefly through social propaganda and social legislation. Whether the immediate object be better housing, better health, better working conditions, better use of leisure, or a long list of other objectives, the main purpose in these different social reforms still is to advance the development of our human kind by improving social relations. Finally, social research, with its precious freight of original discovery in all the fields covered by social work, has also the secondary task of assembling known facts in order to re-interpret them for use in social reform, in group work, and in case work.

I have said earlier that social case work would be only a fragment if separated from the much larger field occupied by social work in general. It is not enough to say this, however; the interdependence of all the parts of social work, or rather the dependence of case work upon these other parts and of these others upon case work, must be illustrated.

As regards the relation between social work with individuals and social work with groups, it should be evident to any one who has read the story in these pages of Miss Sullivan's work with Miss Keller and the six case illustrations following that story, that the intelligent use of community resources, of recreational, educational, and co-operative associations, is the case worker's best indirect means of developing personality. The isolated individual or family is never the normal individual or family. Note, for example, how many community resources were summoned to the assistance of Winifred Jones and her children before that home began to assume a more attractive aspect to its members. There is also a field halfway between case work and group work which, as suggested at the end of Chapter V, might well provide, when better cultivated, new data for social psychology.

No better advice could be given to family case workers, I believe, than to study and develop their work at its point of intersection with social research, with group activities and with social reform or mass betterment. This does not mean that they should drop their work or slight it in order to make special studies or to engage in legislative campaigns, but it does mean that they should be more scientifically productive than they now are, that they should be making social discoveries as a by-product of successful case work (to borrow a phrase of Mrs. Sheffield's), and that they should be bearing faithful witness to the need of social reforms wherever their daily work reveals the need. They should supply the pertinent details necessary during the preliminary period of public education, and help later to make any new legislative measures workable by applying them in their case work.

Two years ago I had occasion to examine a number of outlines of sociology intended as textbooks for college students. Each devoted at least one chapter to the family, but each handled the subject with a polite caution and an absence of first-hand observation which was depressing. The lack of substance in this initial portion of the subject matter of sociology is due not so much to timidity in the authorities as to the almost total absence of case studies which bear upon family life. Here, in this oldest of human institutions, still center the unsolved problems of physical and social heredity and of physical and social environment. Case work cannot solve these problems, of course, but it can develop a fruitful method of approach to their study, and should provide, in time, a body of social data to aid in their solution.

Social discovery is already indebted to family

case work for certain housing reforms and for the first tuberculosis campaigns. It has also had a share, to be indicated later, in child labor reform. But with reference to the internal organization of the family itself, its best work is still to be achieved, though at present there are certain studies in process which should prove helpful, such as the study of marriage laws and marriage law administration previously referred to; such, also, as inquiries bearing upon household management and upon illegitimacy. To these should be added the already published studies of desertion and non-support. There can be no question that family case workers are in an exceptional position to make valuable observations upon family life at first hand where they are protected, as they should be, from too large a case-load, and where they have had the kind of theoretical training in social science and practical training in social work which supplies them with the necessary background. "The interplay," says Professor Park, "of the attractions, tensions, and accommodations of personalities in the intimate bonds of family life have up to the present found no concrete description or adequate analysis in sociological inquiry."* For example, the very phrase "democracy in the family" lacks definition at present, and will continue to lack it until the case method can supply the more specific observation and detail which will develop its meaning.

But what relation can the highly individualized work of the visiting teacher have to social work in general? In the first place, visiting teachers are interpreters of the intent of a whole group of laws, including more especially those for the protection of minors, such as the school attendance and child labor laws. Their service to social reform, like the service of the family case worker, is a reciprocal one, for their work could not go very far without the aid of social legislation. Moreover, "the replies," to quote again from the report published by the New York Public Education Association, "show that visiting teachers have not been content to end their work with the

* Park and Burgess: Introduction to the Science of Sociology, p. 216. Chicago, University of Chicago Press, 1921.

adjustment of individual children, but have drawn conclusions from case work as to general underlying causes and basic changes which should forestall certain maladjustments."*

Again, the child is a social animal, and there is no better way to discover neighborhood conditions and deal with them than to see them first in their effect for good or ill upon some one small person who is responding to them to the very top of his bent. David H. Holbrook tells in *The Family* how the work of a visiting teacher brought new life into those neighborhood activities of a certain district which centered within the school itself. When the mothers, especially the foreign mothers, came to school parties, it was this social worker who knew them and could make them feel at home in the school. Mr. Holbrook asks why such linking together of home and school should be confined to poorer neighborhoods. "When the teachers and patrons of so-called 'better' schools discover what advantages the boys and girls of [other] schools really have through their visiting teachers there will be a

* *Opus cit.*, p. 61.

stampede similar to the rush that finally swept manual training from its early position in classes for mental defectives to an integral part in every school curriculum."*

The hospital social worker is in a peculiarly favorable position, through close association with the medical profession, to aid social reform and social research. The two clinicians—the social and the medical—have their part to play in the prevention of disease and in education for health. Here, too, as in so many other places, prevention, which is sometimes written about as if it were a patent medicine, is neither a thing apart nor a thing substituted, but a most valuable product of the whole process. There is new legislation, for example, designed to control the regulation of communicable and industrial diseases. The practicing physician and the social worker will discover any weaknesses in these new laws by trying to utilize them to the utmost. Gradually they can be amended and, by steady pressure from clinicians, will become a part of the standard of the community.

* *The Family* for February, 1921.

THE FORMS OF SOCIAL WORK

Relations between the judicial function of the presiding officer of a court and the socially interpretative function of the case worker engaged in court service make it especially important that the court worker should know the history of social work and should have a clear grasp, not only of his own special technique, but of its relation to all the other forms of social work. No narrow specialization, no coaching for civil service examinations, can possibly fit him for his responsible task. In fact, it would be difficult to discover the case work field in which the full-time professional worker could fittingly serve without good all-round social work training.

It is natural, I suppose, that closer relations than existed formerly between social work and industrial reform should have begun with the attempt to prevent the premature employment of children. The earlier child labor reform campaigns in this country gave me, as it happens, my first insight into the share that every kind of social work has to take in a genuine and permanent social advance, for progress in the child labor field has been striking, despite the fact that some of our states still lag behind and that the labor of children on farms remains unregulated. The original national program of child labor reform, adopted later in outline, had its inception in the mind of a woman—a social worker belonging to the social and legislative reform group. It won hospitable support at once from neighborhood and settlement workers, and from the social case workers of the country. Sometimes one of these two groups, sometimes the other helped to gather the detailed facts necessary to arouse the public, for such facts were needed, locality by locality. Using in this part of the process whatever elementary knowledge of the technique of social research they happened to have at command, neighborhood and case workers supplied material for pamphlets, leaflets, and newspaper articles. These by-products of individual and neighborhood service would have been of little use, however, without the skill of the social workers specializing in social reform, who provided at this stage the knowledge of how to educate the public, how to draft workable laws, how to conduct legislative campaigns. At the propaganda stage all the different social work groups helped, sometimes against pressure from powerful interests. The social reform group, however, furnished the leadership, and also much of the watchful oversight which has since been necessary.

An important part was borne by the case workers again just after the new child labor measures became law. I know from personal experience in a certain state where there was, at the time, greater industrial demand for the labor of children than in any other, how easily the new child labor law might have been a dead letter save for the devoted service of the case work agencies. For awhile many employers and parents were actively hostile to enforcement, while the administrators of the law were indifferent. The case workers who were my colleagues had to bear more abuse in a good cause than I have known them to be subjected to before or since. But when they undertook to work out, case by case, a reasonable substitute plan for dealing with every instance of alleged hardship—every instance, that is, in which parents claimed that they must have the earnings of a child under fourteen—they were able in co-operation with the local education association to render non-enforcement unnecessary and inexcusable. Wherever, in any state which had passed a child labor law, there were workers in children's societies and family workers "familiar with the homes of the people, habituated to detailed educational processes in those homes, and with the patience to make adjustments, there the assimilation of a new standard [went] forward unchecked."* Where there is no such detailed work going forward quietly from day to day, it often happens that a law upon the statute books which has potential social value is yet no better than a dishonored promissory note.

After this experience I learned to watch for a relation between case work and any given social reform. It has happened again and again, though not always, that case work has preceded and led up to the mass movement by supplying pertinent observations and recorded data. Then

* See a paper of mine, "The Social Case Worker in a Changing World," in the Proceedings of the National Conference of Charities (now National Conference of Social Work) for 1915, p. 48.

later it has followed after the mass movement, and has *applied* the new standard in individual cases at a stage when the application was still difficult. There is a still later stage, as in child labor law enforcement, when social research must be called in to study special phases of the subject—the street trades, for example, or the labor of children in the beet fields. This study must often be undertaken by an agency which continues its work long after the first strongholds of prejudice and inertia have been overcome. Such work is still continued in the national and state Child Labor Committees today, and it must not be assumed that any case work society can become a substitute for such social reform bodies.

It is sometimes claimed that social case workers are not as much interested in bettering the working conditions of adults as they have been in preventing the employment of children. It is true that the direct application of their particular form of skill to adult industry is very recent, but for many years they have been striving to apply the broader principles of industrial justice to their daily tasks. Their attitude toward "relief

in aid of wages" is an example, as shown in the
following passage from an address by Shelby M.
Harrison on Social Case Workers and Better Industrial Conditions:

> I was recently told of the case of a bricklayer who had
> come to one of the charitable societies in New York for
> aid. He was a foreigner, and at the time was not working
> at his trade, but was employed as a porter in one of the
> large downtown buildings. He had a large family, and,
> since his pay was only $12 a week, the children were not
> getting enough to eat. The question before the commit-
> tee was what to do. Four alternatives emerged from the
> discussion: First, the society could supplement the man's
> wages by a regular weekly allowance to the family and let
> him continue at work where he was; second, the society
> might try to get his employer to pay him more wages and
> let him still stay where he was; third, it might try to get
> him back into his trade of bricklaying where he could earn
> a larger wage, the society underwriting the family's needs
> until he should become re-established; fourth, it might
> find him better paying work outside his trade.
>
> It will be seen that any one of the other courses would
> be better than the first. . . . Instead of taking the sim-
> ple and easy course involved in supplementing the man's
> wages, the only course that some of the committee would
> have thought of, it was far more serviceable to the family,
> and impressed an important principle upon that part of
> the committee, when the rule was followed which de-
> clared in effect that "industrial conditions and personal

capacities are far from being as inelastic" as most of us suppose.

The careful consideration of this case brought out other lessons also. It showed that social case workers must be interested in the general mobility of labor; in getting workers into jobs where they can do their best, into places where wages for them are highest relatively or the cost of living lowest. The case worker must think of cases in terms of the whole state or the whole country and consequently must be interested in the many agencies established for the efficient exchange of labor. There may have been still other lessons, but this case will illustrate some of the reasons for urging that the treatment must be on a broad scale and for believing that in so treating them fundamental industrial principles will be taught.*

In his paper Mr. Harrison suggests some of the ways in which case workers can advance public education on industrial questions. They can do this by bearing in mind the industrial facts in cases under treatment, by using single cases to illustrate important industrial principles in the classroom, and by proper emphasis given to the subject in case committees, in the press, and on the platform. Social case records in numbers can also furnish industrial research with clues to be

* Harrison, Shelby M., in Proceedings of the National Conference of Social Work for 1918, p. 305.

followed up, and can serve as a basis for industrial studies made by case work agencies themselves

The public official charged with the enforcement of a law in the successful operation of which no politically influential group in the community is interested, will often find his best backing in a case work agency, whether the law is a new or an old one. Miss Edith Abbott writes:

On two successive committee days in the old West Side office [of the Chicago United Charities] we had the difficult problem of providing for the family of a tubercular man who was doing "light work." One, I remember, was a flagman on the elevated railroad. It occurred to some one to ask for the industrial histories of these men in the hope that some former employer might be found who would assist. Both men had had a history of intermittent light jobs since their physical breakdown, but it appeared when a report was made at a later meeting of the committee that both men had contracted tuberculosis during their employment in the same West Side foundry, where both had worked for a series of years. This interesting fact was promptly reported to a new chief in the Department of Factory Inspection, who promptly investigated this place and found a large number of violations of the so-called "Health, Safety and Comfort law." *

* Abbott, Edith: Paper on "The Social Case Worker and the Enforcement of Industrial Legislation." Proceedings of National Conference of Social Work for 1918, p. 315.

No better service could be rendered by a case work agency than this co-operation with competent but hard pressed public officials. Miss Abbott also gives illustrations in her valuable paper of the useful things that can be done by case workers when public officials are inert and evasive.

It is not so stated in my story, but Rupert Young's original application to a family welfare society* had been made during the panic winter of 1914–15, when he was out of work and had applied for material relief. After consultation with former employers, some assistance was given. A little later Rupert found part time work and, in the stock phrase of social agencies, "the case was closed." The true situation in the Young family and the causes of maladjustment operating at that time which were sure to lead to further trouble later, were not discovered. The failure is fully accounted for. The size of the society's task had increased so rapidly during the panic that it was engaged for the most part in disaster relief work of a necessary but (to the

* See Chapter III.

239

real case worker) most unsatisfactory sort. After that winter was over, industrial conditions, owing to the artificial demand for labor created by the war, changed for the better far more rapidly than is usual after a panic. The plight of Rupert and his wife was again reported to the society in June, 1915, and real social treatment then began. Meanwhile, business had revived and the number of families under the society's care had fallen off —they fell off nearly fifty per cent in the next two years. Judged by totals alone the work that it continued to do might have seemed fifty per cent less necessary, but any one who knows case work also knows that its best and most constructive services were rendered possible by this change to better times. As already stated, none are more eager to see employment regularized than are the case workers. They know better than most that the best remedial service to an unemployed man, absolutely necessary though it is, can be only a poor substitute for his getting real work at real wages; whereas many of the most valuable services of case work, such as those actually achieved in the Young family, have, for lack of time, to be set aside during periods of irregular employment.

Just before the Armistice a distinguished publicist closely identified with various social reforms wrote the following letter, which is quoted by Miss J. C. Colcord in the Proceedings of the National Conference of Social Work for 1919:

For four years we have been without immigration and for two without unemployment, other than seasonal. I hope you are planning a survey which will tell us:

1. How much charity organization work [social case work with families] has been reduced thereby.

2. How much further reduction we may expect from the coming abolition of the liquor traffic.

3. How much additional reduction could be effected by other social and industrial reforms now under consideration.

4. What the irreducible minimum (for the near future) of charity organization work is.*

A fitting reply would have been to submit the summary of Rupert Young's case and of all the cases in Chapter III. It might be argued that, as Rupert was a drinking man, a prohibition amendment was all that was needed to solve his troubles. But, given the conditions of law en-

* See Proceedings, p. 317.

forcement as we find them today in Rupert's own city, it is certain that the amendment alone could not have kept him sober, nor would strict enforcement have met his need, though undoubtedly it would have helped. Moreover, it is a mistake to apply the quantitative test, to ask "how much" in connection with case work, until we know what case work is and why it is, and until we realize fully both its limitations and its possibilities. With regard to the "other social and industrial reforms now under consideration" to which the publicist refers, I can only say with Miss Colcord, "the more the better." Case work is not the rival of any of them or a substitute for any.

This topic of the interplay of different forms of social work deserves fuller treatment than I have been able to give it, but that all forms are inextricably interwoven in the great task of furthering social advance should be evident. A colleague of mine who was examining a group of applicants for certain positions complained that too many of them were oversupplied with slogans and undersupplied with the technical details of the task to be done. As a matter of fact, there can be no solid advance without patient attention to detail or without respect for workmanship. Unhappily a certain contempt for technique often lurks behind a glib use of catch-words and high-sounding phrases. On the other hand, the professional worker who, in any field, has imagination enough to deal effectively with concrete things, to scrutinize them and "put them together without abstraction," is also likely to be the one who can be trusted to see their larger relations. The great technicians, like Osler in medicine and Pasteur in chemistry, have been men highly sensitive to the relations of the part to the whole.

As one of the newest of the professions, social work should strive to hold an even balance between the specializing and the generalizing tendencies. In its training schools, it must develop a sound technique under instructors who know at first hand the practice of its different specialties. In a strong professional organization, national in scope, it must be able to hold all the forms of social work together and steadily enlarge that well-cultivated field which is occupied by all in common.

XI

CASE WORK AND DEMOCRACY

IN MIDDLEMARCH, Dr. Lydgate expresses this view of his work: "I should never have been happy in any profession that did not call forth the highest intellectual strain, and yet keep me in good warm contact with my neighbors." Social case workers have this same feeling about their task. Their profession is an arduous one, but it puts upon each practitioner the highest intellectual strain of which he is capable, while his contacts with the human side of life are warm, continuous, and richly rewarding.

Those who began years ago, in some of the family welfare agencies and children's aid societies, to develop a method of dealing with disadvantaged families and with dependent children—a method which took personal and social possibilities more fully into account than had previously been the case—entered upon their task with the courage and devotion of pioneers. They had no other end in view, however, than to do their best for clients A and B and C; their sole purpose was to give these socially handicapped individuals a square deal. Working out faithfully this legitimate and necessary aim, they did not realize that they were also helping to build some of the foundations of essential justice for the democracy of the future.

The earlier case work, in the light of our accumulated experience, often seems crude, but modern case workers should realize that their own labors, while aiding new discovery now, may some day make a like impression upon their successors. Not any more devotedly, but more clear-sightedly, perhaps, than formerly, they can attack each new difficulty against a background of total social purpose. That sense of the whole of social work to which I have referred more than once can now be an ever-present reality.

An important part of that whole is the service which social work can render in the field of public administration. It must be evident from my discussion of individual differences in Chapter VI and from the brief outline in the chapter preceding this one, describing the different fields of social work, that the strengthening of public administration seems to me one of the great ends which every form of social endeavor must have in view. But it is possible to move toward that end and transfer the special contributions of social work into government keeping with such ill-considered haste that, when they arrive at their destination, the label minus the contents is all that remains. As this preliminary examination of case work draws to its close, I should like to add a few words to what has already been said about the relation of social work, and of case work more especially, to democracy.

Every few years, inspired in part by some realization of the present day weaknesses of public administration and in part by a narrow view of what constitutes democracy, some one makes the discovery that all the activities of social work should be absorbed by the state. Others of us, who feel that the state is only one of the desirable forms of association in a free society and that the right of voluntary association is a safeguard against autocracy, are not enthusiastic about placing under the state every item in so wide and varied a group of functions, though we recognize that the auspices under which any given form of social work—case work, for example—continues to make headway will have to change from time to time. Whether or not these changes mean, as they probably will and should, that certain case work tasks initiated privately and still under private management are to become public functions later, all will agree that the important thing is for social work to be ready for changes to governmental control before they arrive. Sometimes, as we have already seen in these pages, public departments and institutions have adopted case work policies in name only, because it was not possible at the time to supply the necessary skill for their execution or possible to control the size of the task. Lacking that control, pressure of numbers meant low standards of service and no permanent results. This has not always been the outcome, but those who believe most sincerely in the extension of case work and its extension under both public and voluntary control are most anxious to see each advance effected under conditions that assure something better than failure.

Under whatever auspices case work is destined to go forward, a respect for personality will be essential. Such respect implies a democratic point of view. Social case work cannot progress under those who have the autocratic spirit. But is that spirit to be avoided by transforming all our social agencies into government bureaus over night? Not the one or the other, but both public and private auspices will continue to be necessary, though there is the third possibility that some social case workers will develop a private, independent practice of their own. The public agency must be able to assure some degree of continuity of policy, free from political party control, before case workers will enter its service gladly and in large numbers. When this condition is fulfilled, certain forms of case work may well make greater advances and certainly serve a larger clientele under public management than under private. The privately supported agency, on the other hand, which already gives fair assurance of continuity of policy, must make itself more attractive to skilled social workers by giving staff members a larger measure of representation upon its administrative committees.

Democracy, however, is not a form of organization but a daily habit of life. It is not enough for social workers to speak the language of democracy; they must have in their hearts its spiritual conviction of the infinite worth of our common humanity before they can be fit to do any form of social work whatsoever. Life itself achieves significance and value not from the esoteric things shared by the few, but from the great common experiences of the race—from the issues of birth and death, of affection satisfied and affection frustrated, from those chances and hazards of daily living that come to all men. Unless these conditions common to all humanity strongly appeal to us, or until they do, we are not ready to adopt social case work as our major interest.

For the last eleven years it has been my privilege to conduct every spring an informal institute of members selected from among the professional case workers in some of the family welfare societies of the country. As these groups have been chosen throughout the whole period on the same basis, changes in institute personnel during the eleven years have been a rough but fair index of what is happening to case work in the family agencies. The best element in the institute of 1921 was no better than the best in the institute of 1910; but no longer is there a wide gap between the most and the least able. In recent years, the spirit and ability of the whole group has been excellent, and their leader can testify that there is no lack of democracy among them.

Another interesting fact to be observed in the field of professional social work is the increasing demand for well trained case workers, whether in the children's, the family, or the medical field. In some branches of social work there have been fluctuations in the demand, dependent upon whether times were good or bad, or the period was one of war or peace. But for social case workers who can do their work well the demand has continued to be far greater than the supply.

The supremely important question today is not

the extension of case work activities to larger fields, though extension is undoubtedly a goal, and not whether such work should be publicly or privately supported at present, but whether it can be assured freedom of growth—freedom to do good work and freedom to make new discovery through intensive service. It is the intensive, long continued case work of which I have tried to give a few examples in this book that holds within itself the seeds of future development, the seeds of greater knowledge of the human material with which it so venturesomely deals and greater knowledge of the true relation of man to society. The widest possible applications of case work to life can only follow, they cannot precede, the findings of its best practitioners; and these findings, valuable as they have already become, are only the first fruits of what promises to be a bountiful harvest.

It follows that one of the great, unused opportunities to serve humanity and further social progress lies in the endowment of special ability in this particular field. I would not plead for any permanent endowment, but for a large sum to be expended in our own day and time in releasing thoroughly tested and exceptionally gifted case workers from pressure of overwork, and thus enable them to render a better grade of service. A small band of students (not more than four at any one time) might serve under these selected leaders, who would be making careful note of the results of one method and another, and of the conditions under which each had been tried.

The six women who did the work described in Chapters II and III live in different cities. Most of them do not know and have never even heard of one another. They have no adequate time at present in which to think, to study, or to discover what people are doing in other places. All their time is given to keeping abreast of the arduous day's work. To release earnest, devoted people such as these from some of the details of their task, to double their usefulness by cutting the volume of their present work in half, would enable them to build a solid foundation of skill and detailed knowledge for the whole profession, would enrich the social resources of the world at a strategic point.

The gains already made in case work are significant and inspiring. They have been made against heavy odds, and the faith and courage that have gone into them deserve the kind of recognition here suggested—a kind which in medicine has already brought such rich returns. It is fully recognized that endowment of special ability in the fields of scientific research and of education has been a way of advancing public welfare from which every one has been the gainer. Similar endowments in the field of the study and practical adjustment of social relations would serve not alone certain socially disadvantaged groups, but all humanity.

We are told that the law is no respecter of persons. Be that as it may, we are slowly realizing that administrators of the law—not in courts alone but in a hundred places where it is a question of carrying out the intent of the law—must learn to interpret that intent through respect for personality. Wherever these administrators ignore the things that help and hinder personality, wherever they fail to study and allow for individual differences, treating unequal things

253

equally instead, the intent of the law and its actual achievement become so little related that they often appear to glide by one another like ships that pass in the night. Social advance could not be better served than by such a series of discoveries and training processes as would give this country a new generation of administrators—a generation skilled in adapting the public intent to the individual circumstances.

XII

CONCLUSION

LET ME now attempt to sum up in a few paragraphs the ground which has been covered in the preceding pages of introductory description.

Examples of social case work show that, by direct and indirect insights, and direct and indirect action upon the minds of clients, their social relations can be improved and their personalities developed.

Insights imply a knowledge of innate make-up and of the effects of environment upon the individual. The failure of a case worker to learn his client's social and personal background usually means failure to effect any permanent adjustment, but these diagnostic processes interplay with those of treatment, and no sharp line can be drawn between them.

Action ranges from the humblest services, guided by affection, patience, and personal sympathy, to such radical measures as complete change of environment, the organization of resources where none existed before, and the reknitting of ties long broken. Officialism is to be avoided. The most successful case work policies are encouragement and stimulation, the fullest possible participation of the client in all plans, and the skilful use of repetition. Sometimes there must be warning and discipline; always there must be direct action of mind on mind. One of the most characteristic methods of case work is its many-sided approach, its assembling, binding together, and readjusting processes. The social case worker is not, however, a sort of benevolent middleman. It is true that he acts through other specialists, other agencies, and through his client's own social group, but, in bringing people together, he is far from washing his hands of the consequences of the contacts effected; on the contrary, he is deeply concerned to discover, with all these others, a joint program which shall achieve the desired social result. It is the combination of all these enumerated services, or of most of them and not of any one or two, which constitutes social case work of professional grade.

No case worker is bound to accept the philosophy of any other, but a philosophy of some kind he must have. The foundation stones of such a philosophy are suggested in this book; they are given, however, with the fullest realization that other and even more fundamental ones may soon be revealed. These suggested foundations, to restate them informally, are as follows:

(1) Human beings are interdependent. There is a spiritual unity about this conception which means a great deal to those who have grasped its full meaning and are trying to live by it. Professor MacIver tells us that "society is best ordered when it best promotes the personality of its members." The converse is also true. We achieve personality through right relations to society and in no other way. The art of social case work is the art of discovering and assuring to the individual the best possible social relations.

(2) Human beings are different. A genuinely democratic social program equalizes opportunity by intelligent mass action, and provides at the

same time for an administrative policy which does different things for and with different people.

(3) Human beings are not dependent and domestic animals. This fact of man's difference from other animals establishes the need of his participation in making and carrying out plans for his welfare. Individuals have wills and purposes of their own and are not fitted to play a passive part in the world; they deteriorate when they do.

Perhaps this is why men and women who are to become assets to society must have had a careful preparation for that network of interrelations which we call life. They cannot be turned out at wholesale. In recognition of the fact that the making of a social person takes time and detailed attention, the home is the social institution to which is usually entrusted the beginnings of this task, and it is in the home that the first case work adjustments were attempted. The workshop is another place in which the case work method is destined to effect beneficent changes, though its introduction there is recent and not yet fully developed. Wherever case work becomes a serviceable adjunct of some other and older profession, as in the social institutions of the school, the hospital, and the court, it is even more important than elsewhere that its practitioners should be thoroughly grounded in their own specialty before attempting to supplement the work of other specialists.

The whole of social work is greater than any of its parts. All parts serve personality, but in different ways. Case work serves it by effecting better adjustments between individuals and their social environment; group work serves it by dealing with people face to face but no longer one by one; social reform serves it by effecting mass betterment through propaganda and social legislation; and social research serves personality by making original discoveries and re-interpreting known facts for the use of these other forms of social work. The case worker should know something of all forms—the more knowledge he has of all the better—and should carry through his special task in such a way as to advance all of the types of social work just enumerated.

Finally, the highest test of social case work is growth in personality. Does the personality of its clients change, and change in the right direction? Is energy and initiative released, that is, in the direction of higher and better wants and saner social relations? Only an instinctive reverence for personality, and a warm human interest in people as people can win for the social case worker an affirmative answer to this question. But an affirmative answer means growth in personality for the case worker himself. The service is reciprocal.

INDEX

Abbott, Edith, 196, 238

Action, direct, of mind on mind, 102, 107–110; indirect, through the social environment, 102, 110–121

Adjustment: between the individual and his social environment will always be necessary, 98; out of, 134

Adler, Felix, 150, 171–172, 184

Administrators of the law, 253–254

Aimless dosings of social ills, 87

Allegri, Lucia: story of, 80–86; case of, cited, 107, 109, 114, 117, 118, 119, 120, 121, 139

Allowance, regular weekly, 73

Almshouse worker quoted, 127

Americanization, 118, 154

American Marriage Laws, 183 (footnote)

Analysis of acts and policies in six case illustrations, 101–121

Applicant, term not used in case work, 28 (footnote)

Arbitrariness avoided, 40

Arnold, Matthew, 195

Associated Charities. See *Family Welfare Societies*

Atonement and Personality. R. C. Moberly, D.D., 94 (footnote)

Attendance officers, 219

Autocracy: in the policy of the same thing for everybody, 150; case work cannot progress under an, 248

Background of husband and wife, differences in, 56

Back history, 33–34, 70, 76, 80, 83, 106, 137

Baldwin, James Mark, 129–130, 171

Basset, a Village Chronicle. S. G. Tallentyre, 6

Begging, 60

Belonging, the sense of, 119, 189

Bielowski, Maria: story of, 31–43; case of, cited, 96, 105–106, 108, 109, 112, 114, 116, 118, 119, 122–124, 217

Biography and the study of family life, 190–194

Blind: the greatest single handicap of the, 161–162

Boarding homes, 44

Bojer, Johan, 126

Bosanquet, Mrs. Bernard, 163

Breaking up the home, 72

Breckenridge, Sophonisba P., 196

Bridgman, Laura, 7, 9, 15

Laura Bridgman, Dr. Howe's Famous Pupil. Maud Howe and Florence Howe Hall, 7

Broken Homes. Joanna C. Colcord, 155

Bronner, Dr. Augusta, 105 (footnote)

Brooks, Phillips, 20

Campbell, Dr. F. J., 161–162

Cannon, Ida M., 213

Case: a term applied to the situation, not the person, 27

Case conferences, 136–137

INDEX

Case records: Dr. Howe's, 8, 10, 28; Miss Sullivan's letters, 10; choice of, 26–31; uses of, 28–30; confidential nature of, 29

Case Work and Democracy, 244–254. See also *Social Case Work*

Causal factors, search for, 79

Change of environment, 13, 24, 43, 53, 66, 116–118, 198

Charity organization societies. See *Family Welfare Societies*

Child labor: 76; campaigns, 203, 231–235; committees, 235

Child-placing societies: work of, with George Foster, 43–49; early case work in, 244–245

Child welfare work: fuller records of, 30–31; illustrations of, 26–49; and daily life, 177; for neglected and difficult children, 219; in child labor campaigns, 234

Children: building upon affection for, 58, 61, 66–67; the rights of, 181, 186, 188

Choosing illustrations, process of, 26–31

Church attendance, 113

Client, use of the term, in case work, 27

Club work, 223

Colcord, Joanna C., 155, 241, 242

Combination of many itemized insights and acts involved in case work of professional grade, 102, 124

Community resources: 15, 16, 18, 19; case workers' duty in the absence of, 115; utilization of, by case workers, 225

Community work, 223

Conclusion, 255–260

Confidential nature: of case histories, 29; of relation of social worker to client, 29

Conklin, Edwin Grant, 146

Continuity of policy, 248

Court: decision based on social evidence, 42; probation officer and, 123; children's rights in the, 188; probation in the, 216–217; procedure in the, 215, 217; social evidence in the, of the future, 218

Criminal Justice in Cleveland. Pound and Frankfurter, 215

Criticism of case work processes on basis of long-term, intensive treatment, 90

Definition, a tentative, of social case work, 98; basis of, 87–90

Democracy: and individual difference, 149–154; in the family, 182, 228; case work and, 244–254, 248–249; a daily habit of life, 249

Dewey, John, 142 (footnote)

Difficult girl, a, 31–43; Teresa Allegri, 83

Disasters and rehabilitation, 219

Discipline, 12–13, 22, 64, 109

Drinking man, 51–59

Drinking woman, 59–68

Dutcher, Elizabeth, 110

Elements of Social Science, The. R. M. MacIver, 95 (footnote)

Eliot, George, 214, 244

Employers, 119–120

Endowment of special ability in the social case work field, 251–254

Enuresis, 35

Environment: 22, 23; social and physical, distinguished, 99; heredity versus, 146–149. See also *Change of* and *Social*

Equality: not likeness, 150; the essence of, 151

Ethical Philosophy of Life, An. Felix Adler, 150

Eugenics, 148–149

INDEX

Evolution and Ethics. Thomas Huxley, 128

Expert advice, 20, 24

Face of the World, The. Johan Bojer, 126

Family, the: a council of, 84–86; personal equation in discussions of, 177–178; specialists should know facts of the life of, 180; children the test of, 181; that fails, 187–188; as a test of industrial organization, 201–202; in current outlines of sociology, 226. See also *The Home*

Family deserters, 135, 154–155

Family Social Work, Institute of, 249–250

Family welfare societies: fuller records of, 30–31; case work of, illustrated, 51–86, 134–136, 139–142, 185; and housing, 227; and tuberculosis campaigns, 227; and studies of desertion and non-support, 227; and social research, 227–228; in child labor campaigns, 232–234; early case work in, 244–245; an index of what is happening in, 250

Fathers and Children. Ivan Turgenev, 187

Feeble-minded, the, 55, 111, 182

Finding work, 206–210

Follett, M. P., 145

Forms of Social Work, the, 222–243

Foster, George, story of, 43–49; case of, cited, 96, 110, 112, 116, 179, 189

Foster homes, selection of, 44

Frankness, 21, 40

Free homes, selection of, 44

Freedom of growth the important thing in case work, 251

Fundamental principles restated, 257–258

Group character of some case treatment, 80, 111, 139–142

Group thinking, 84–86

Group work, 223, 224, 229

Habit, re-education of, 73, 108

Haldane, J. S., 95 (footnote)

Hall, Florence Howe, 7

Hamilton, Cicely, 178

Handicapped, work with, 220

Harrison, Shelby M., 236

Health, see *Physical Condition*

Healy, Dr. Wm., 104 (footnote), 121

Heath, Arthur George, 165

Heredity and Environment. Edwin Grant Conklin, 146

Heredity versus environment, 146–149

Hocking, Wm. Ernest, 132

Holbrook, David H., 229

Home, the, 175–194; developing affection for, 58; re-established, 63; instinct of, 65; breaking up, 72; as a family center, 78; and children, 118; not the institution of, for its own sake, 179; many kinds of social work visits to, 180; proposed substitutes for, 181; and the school, 197; and the workshop, 201–202; rehabilitation of, after disasters, 219; as a preparation for life, 258. See also *The Family*

Hospital social work, 210–214, 230

Housing conditions, 120–121

Howe, Maud, 7

Howe, Dr. Samuel Gridley, 7–9, 10

Human Interdependence, 126–143, 257

Human Nature and Its Remaking. Wm. Ernest Hocking, 132

Human Psychology. Howard C. Warren, 94 (footnote)

INDEX

Humble services as a means of treatment, 23, 58, 64, 107–108

Husband and wife disagree, 51–59, 184

Huxley, Thos., 127–128

Illustrations: Miss Sullivan and Helen Keller, 9–25; process of choosing, 26–31; Maria Bielowski, a difficult girl, 31–43; George Foster, a dependent child placed out, 43–49; Mr. and Mrs. Rupert Young, husband and wife who cannot agree, 51–59; Clara Vansca and her neglected children, 59–68; Winifred Jones and her children, widow not an efficient home maker, 68–80; Lucia Allegri and her relatives, who fail to understand her situation, 80–86; pellagra cases, 134–135; desertion case, 135–136; group case work, 139–142; unwise service, 167–171; of visiting teaching, 199–200; of case work in compensation field, 205–206; relief in aid of wages, 236; reports to public departments, 238

Imaginative sympathy, 23, 37, 42, 106, 107

Immigrant family, 80–86, 185–186

Immigration: 117–118; recent, 154; and case work, 220–221

Individual Differences, 144–158, 257–258

Industrial: employment of women and equality, 152–153; conditions, 237

Industrial disease legislation, 230

Infallibility, no claim of, 40

Innate make-up: and prognoses, 105 (footnote); not easily distinguished, 145

Insight into individuality and social environment, 101–102, 103–107

Instinctive responses versus the reasoning and habit-forming processes, 164

Institutional care, 43, 60, 189

Intensive case work, 90, 142, 176, 251

Interest, any serious, has power of radiation, 136

Interrelation of the different forms of social work, 222–243

Introduction, 5–25

Introduction to the Science of Sociology. Park and Burgess, 228

Irresponsibility, 57

James, William, 191

Jones, Winifred: story of, 68–80; case of, cited, 104, 108, 112, 113, 114, 117, 119, 121, 166, 179, 189, 225

Keeping faith, 24, 108

Keller, Helen, 10–25

Knowing what is happening, 41

Kropotkin, Prince, 129

Lane, Franklin K., 203

Legal aid societies, 220

Letters of William James, The. Edited by his son, 191

Level of participation, 170

Life of Pasteur, The. René Valery-Radot, 192–194

Lippmann, Walter, 142 (footnote)

Long-term services to individuals, 90, 142, 176, 251

MacIver, R. M., 95 (footnote), 146

Macy, Mrs., see Sullivan

Marital difficulties, 52–59

Mark, Thistleton, 95 (footnote)

Marriage: current discussions of, 177; the rights of children and, 181; laws relating to, 182; administration of, laws, 183, 227; education for, 184–185

INDEX

Marriage and Divorce. Felix Adler, 184

Mead, George M., 130

Mechanism, Life and Personality. J. S. Haldane, 95 (footnote)

Medical-social work, 210–214; pressure of numbers in, 212–213

Mendelian laws and human inheritance, 147

Mental examination, 72, 112

Mental experts, 106

Mental hygiene: of industrial workers, 204

Mental testing, 46; value of, 104 (footnote); and social evidence, 72, 104–105

Meredith, George, 183

Meyer, Dr. Adolf, 183

Moberly, R. C., D.D., 94 (footnote)

Moral and Social Significance of the Conception of Personality. Arthur George Heath, 165

Motive, 170–171

Mutual Aid, a Factor in Evolution. Prince Kropotkin, 129

Myerson, Dr. Abraham, 147

Neglected children, 59–68

Neighborhood: opportunities of a new, 66; work, 223; conditions, 229

New generation of administrators, 254

New State, The. M. P. Follett, 145

Numbers, pressure of: in visiting teaching, 200; in hospital social work, 212–213; in family social work, 208, 210, 227, 239–241; in probation work, 217; in public service, 247; in all forms of social case work, 252

Obedience, lessons in, 12–13, 22

Occupational resources, 119–120

Officialism, absence of, 108

Osler, Sir William, 243

Our Social Heritage. Graham Wallas, 148, 153

Outlines of Historical Jurisprudence. Sir Paul Vinogradoff, 202

Panic year, figures of a, 51

Parent: and child, 160, 185; obligations to, 187

Park, Robert E., 227

Parole officers, 220

Participation of the client in making and carrying out plans for his welfare, 39, 48, 109–110, 170–171, 173

Pasteur, Louis, 192–194, 243

Patience, 108

Pauperism, 167

Pearson, Sir Arthur, 162

Pedagogy and personality, 94 (footnote)

Pellagra, 135

Perkins, Frances, 204–206

Perkins Institution for the Blind, 7, 9, 19

Permanent welfare as a test of case work, 90, 142

Perry, Bliss, 93 (footnote)

Personal equation, the, in discussions of the family, 177–178

Personal influence, 108

Personal side of case work, 126–128, 244

Personality: of Helen Keller, 22; the service of, 24–25; development of, the aim of case work, 90, 97, 260; effect of loss of social status or health upon, 91; nature of, 92; and individual differences, 92; must grow or atrophy, 93; no scale for measuring, 121–122; not static, 122, 131; society the source and origin of, 129–132, 257; reverence for, 158, 248; all forms of social work serve, 259

Philosophy of social case work, 128, 257

Physical condition, 35, 46, 48, 54, 57, 63, 74, 79, 112, 141

Physicians: and social case work, 135, 144; and patients, 160; private practice of, 221

Pity, the handicap of an unnerving, 161–162

Placement work, 37, 44–49

Plato on equality, 151

Pound, Roscoe, 215

Prevention, 230

Preventive medicine, 211

Principles of Sociology. E. A. Ross, 185

Privately supported agencies: staff representation in, 248–249; continuity of policy in, 248

Probation: for Maria Bielowski, 32–35, 42; insights needed in, 122–123; pressure of numbers in, 216–217; need of good social training for, work, 231

Professional organization of social workers, national in scope, 243

Prohibition, 241–242

Psychiatric Family Studies. Dr. Abraham Myerson, 147

Psychiatry and social case work, 133, 144, 213, 221

Psychology from the Standpoint of a Behaviorist. J. B. Watson, 94 (footnote), 164–165

Public administration and case work, 238–239, 245–248, 253–254

Public Education Association of New York, 198, 200, 228

Public employment bureaus, 207

Purposeful Action: the Basis of, 159–174; routine and, 164

Recreation, 37, 68, 73, 114, 223

Reid, Thomas, 91

Relatives, 12; participation of, in case work, 16; of Rupert Young, 53–59; of Clara Vansca, 62, 65, 113; of Winifred Jones, 69, 77; of Lucia Allegri, 84, 85; of a button maker's family, 140

Relief, material: 167–174; as a substitute for justice, 172; in aid of wages, 236–237

Religious instruction, 20–21, 24, 113, 144

Repetition, 75, 109, 166

Rigidity, no permanence with extreme of, 184

Ross, E. A., 184–185

Royce, Josiah, 130

Sainte-Beuve, Charles-Augustin, 222

School records, 45, 48, 66, 74, 112, 169

School — Workshop — Hospital —Court, 195–221

Schools: policy of same thing for everybody in, 196; case work in, 196–201

Self-respect, appeal to, 38

Sense of the whole in social work, 223, 245, 259

Sham families, 187–188

Shopmates, co-operation of, 140

Short-term services to individuals, 88, 176

Social agencies, team play between, 113–114, 141

Social Case Work: in Being, 26–86; defined, 87–125; unconscious, 5–7, 11; as neighborliness, 7; when subsidiary to some other professional service, 27, 88–89, 214, 259; widening scope of, 30, 251; profession of, not well established, 87 (footnote); of the short-term variety, 88, 176; of the long-term and intensive type, 89–90, 142, 176, 251; a form of teaching, 94, 96; the special approach of, 96; distinguished from mass treatment, 98; is, a specialized form of skill? 100; material with which, deals a part of daily life, 102, 177; personal side of, 126–128, 244; must have a philosophy, 128, 257; and psychiatry, 133, 144, 213, 221; of one, two, and three dimensions, 138–142; and social psychology, 142–143; field of, not identical with that of other professions dealing with personality, 144; and reverence for personality, 158; present-day, 175; intensive, may bear a separate name later, 176; short-term, 176; in schools, 196–201; in workshops, 204; in hospitals, 210–214; in courts, 216; private practice of, 221; and group work, 224; and social reforms, 225, 234; and social research, 227, 230; in child labor campaigns, 232–234; and industrial conditions, 237; and public officials, 238; under public and private auspices, 248

Social case workers, increasing demand for, 250

Social diagnosis, skill in, saves time, 103–104

Social environment: 99; insight into the resources, dangers, and influence of the, 102, 103–107; approach through the, characteristic of case work, 111; indirect action through the, illus., 139–142

Social and Ethical Interpretations in Mental Development. James Mark Baldwin, 130

Social heritage, 147–149

Social psychology and social case work, 142–143

Social reform, 223, 227, 228, 231

Social relationship: no one, can serve for all, 111; a key to client's life, 132; the approach by way of, 133–134

Social research, 224, 227, 230, 251–253

Social settlements, 143, 223, 232

Social Work in Hospitals. Ida M. Cannon, 213 (footnote)

Social work and social case work, 115

Society the source and origin of personality, 129–132

Special ability, endowment of, 251–254

Spiritual gains, 20–21, 68

Staff representation on committees of private agencies, 249

Stages of development: in social case work, 154; in medicine, 211; in the administration of justice, 215

Standard of Life, The. Mrs. Bernard Bosanquet, 163

Stimulation: and encouragement, program of, 72, 75, 80, 109; of wants, 166

Story of My Life, The. Helen Keller, 11–22

Stout, G. F., 162

Stranded travelers, 220

Studies in Good and Evil. Josiah Royce, 130

Study of Poetry, A. Bliss Perry, 93 (footnote)

Subsidiary case work, supplementing service of another profession, 27, 88–89, 214, 259

Suggestion, 73

Sullivan, Anne Mansfield (Mrs. Macy), 9–25, 40, 95, 107, 117, 224

Summary of ground covered, 255–260

Sympathy, two kinds of, 23; imaginative, 37, 42

Syphilis, 35, 41

Tallentyre, S. G., 6

Teacher and pupil, 160

Teaching and social case work, 95, 133, 144

Technique: and constructive imagination, 107; versus slogans, 242; and a sense of the whole, 243

Temperament, 91 (footnote)

Thrift, lessons in, 64–65, 67, 114

Trade union a serious interest, 136

Trained social workers, need of, 157, 251

Training schools of social work, 243

Truancy and Non-Attendance in the Chicago Schools. Abbott and Breckenridge, 196

Trust estates, administration of, a field for social case work, 219

Tuberculosis, 140

Turgenev, Ivan, 187

Unemployed, the, 154, 208–210, 239–242

Unfavorable conditions, 165–166

Unfit, the, 127–128, 182

Unfolding of Personality, the, as the Chief Aim of Education. Thistleton Mark, 95 (footnote)

Unwise service, 167–171

Vaile, Gertrude, 150–151

Vallery-Radot, René, 194

Van Dyke, Dr. Henry, 151

Vansca, Clara, story of, 59–68; case of, cited, 108, 109, 113, 114, 116, 118, 119, 121, 179

Victory Over Blindness. Sir Arthur Pearson, 162

Vinogradoff, Sir Paul, 202

Visiting Teacher in the United States, The. A survey by the National Association of Visiting Teachers and Home and School Visitors, 200

Visiting teachers, 197–201, 228

Vocational guidance, 206, 220

Wallas, Graham, 147–148, 153

Wants: stimulation of, 166; progressive and higher, 167

Warren, Howard C., 94 (footnote)

Watson, J. B., 94 (footnote), 164

Wider self, theory of the, 131

Widow with children, 68–80

Working homes, 36, 44

Workmen's compensation administration and case work, 204–206

Workshop, the: and the home, 201–202; case work in, 204, 220

Young, Mr. and Mrs. Rupert, story of, 51–59; case of, cited, 108, 110, 112, 113, 116, 118, 120, 121, 210, 239–242

POVERTY, U. S. A.

THE HISTORICAL RECORD

An Arno Press/New York Times Collection

Adams, Grace. **Workers on Relief.** 1939.

The Almshouse Experience: Collected Reports. 1821-1827.

Armstrong, Louise V. **We Too Are The People.** 1938.

Bloodworth, Jessie A. and Elizabeth J. Greenwood.
The Personal Side. 1939.

Brunner, Edmund de S. and Irving Lorge.
**Rural Trends in Depression Years: A Survey of
Village-Centered Agricultural Communities, 1930-1936.**
1937.

Calkins, Raymond.
**Substitutes for the Saloon: An Investigation Originally
made for The Committee of Fifty.** 1919.

Cavan, Ruth Shonle and Katherine Howland Ranck.
**The Family and the Depression: A Study of
One Hundred Chicago Families.** 1938.

Chapin, Robert Coit.
**The Standard of Living Among Workingmen's Families
in New York City.** 1909.

**The Charitable Impulse in Eighteenth Century America:
Collected Papers.** 1711-1797.

Children's Aid Society.
Children's Aid Society Annual Reports, 1-10.
February 1854-February 1863.

Conference on the Care of Dependent Children.
**Proceedings of the Conference on the Care
of Dependent Children.** 1909.

Conyngton, Mary.
How to Help: A Manual of Practical Charity. 1909.

Devine, Edward T. **Misery and its Causes.** 1909.

Devine, Edward T. **Principles of Relief.** 1904.

Dix, Dorothea L.
On Behalf of the Insane Poor: Selected Reports. 1843-1852.

Douglas, Paul H.
**Social Security in the United States: An Analysis and
Appraisal of the Federal Social Security Act.** 1936.

Farm Tenancy: Black and White. Two Reports. 1935, 1937.

Feder, Leah Hannah.
**Unemployment Relief in Periods of Depression:
A Study of Measures Adopted in Certain American
Cities, 1857 through 1922.** 1936.

Folks, Homer.
**The Care of Destitute, Neglected, and
Delinquent Children.** 1900.

Guardians of the Poor.
**A Compilation of the Poor Laws of the State of
Pennsylvania from the Year 1700 to 1788, Inclusive.** 1788.

Hart, Hastings, H.
Preventive Treatment of Neglected Children.
(Correction and Prevention, Vol. 4) 1910.

Herring, Harriet L.
**Welfare Work in Mill Villages: The Story of Extra-Mill
Activities in North Carolina.** 1929.

The Jacksonians on the Poor: Collected Pamphlets.
1822-1844.

Karpf, Maurice J.
Jewish Community Organization in the United States.
1938.

Kellor, Frances A.
Out of Work: A Study of Unemployment. 1915.

Kirkpatrick, Ellis Lore.
The Farmer's Standard of Living. 1929.

Komarovsky, Mirra.
The Unemployed Man and His Family: The Effect of Unemployment Upon the Status of the Man in Fifty-Nine Families. 1940.

Leupp, Francis E. **The Indian and His Problem.** 1910.

Lowell, Josephine Shaw.
Public Relief and Private Charity. 1884.

More, Louise Bolard.
Wage Earners' Budgets: A Study of Standards and Cost of Living in New York City. 1907.

New York Association for Improving the Condition of the Poor.
AICP First Annual Reports Investigating Poverty. 1845-1853.

O'Grady, John.
Catholic Charities in the United States: History and Problems. 1930.

Raper, Arthur F.
Preface to Peasantry: A Tale of Two Black Belt Counties. 1936.

Raper, Arthur F. **Tenants of The Almighty.** 1943.

Richmond, Mary E.
What is Social Case Work? An Introductory Description. 1922.

Riis, Jacob A. **The Children of the Poor.** 1892.

Rural Poor in the Great Depression: Three Studies. 1938.

Sedgwick, Theodore.
Public and Private Economy: Part I. 1836.

Smith, Reginald Heber. **Justice and the Poor.** 1919.

Sutherland, Edwin H. and Harvey J. Locke.
Twenty Thousand Homeless Men: A Study of Unemployed Men in the Chicago Shelters. 1936.

Tuckerman, Joseph.
On the Elevation of the Poor: A Selection From His Reports as Minister at Large in Boston. 1874.

Warner, Amos G. **American Charities.** 1894.

Watson, Frank Dekker.
The Charity Organization Movement in the United States: A Study in American Philanthropy. 1922.

Woods, Robert A., et al. **The Poor in Great Cities.** 1895.